EIGHTEENTH DYNASTY
BEFORE THE
AMARNA PERIOD

INSTITUTE OF RELIGIOUS ICONOGRAPHY
STATE UNIVERSITY GRONINGEN

ICONOGRAPHY OF RELIGIONS

EDITED BY

TH. P. VAN BAAREN, L. P. VAN DEN BOSCH, L. LEERTOUWER, F. LEEMHUIS,
H. TE VELDE, H. WITTE, AND H. BUNING (*Secretary*)

SECTION XVI: EGYPT

FASCICLE FIVE

LEIDEN
E. J. BRILL
1985

EIGHTEENTH DYNASTY BEFORE THE AMARNA PERIOD

BY

KAROL MYŚLIWIEC

LEIDEN
E. J. BRILL
1985

ISBN 90 04 07028 1

CONTENTS

Bibliography and Sources of Photographs.. VII

Introduction 1

Catalogue of Illustrations 31

Plates I—XLVIII

BIBLIOGRAPHY

ABITZ F., Statuetten in Schreinen als Grabbeigaben in den ägyptischen Königsgräbern der 18. und 19. Dynastie, ÄA 35, Wiesbaden, 1979.

ABUBAKR A. E. M. J., Untersuchungen über die ägyptischen Kronen, Glückstadt-Hamburg-New York, 1937.

ACHIERY H. EL, BARGUET P., DEWACHTER M., Le temple d'Amada. Cahier I. Architecture, Le Caire, 1967.

ACHIERY H. EL, ALY M., DEWACHTER M., Le Speos d'El-Lessiya. Cahier II. Plans d'architecture. Dessins. Index, Le Caire, 1968.

ALY M., ABDEL HAMID F., DEWACHTER M., Le Temple d'Amada. Cahier IV. Dessins, Tables de concordance, Le Caire, 1967.

ARNOLD D., Wandrelief und Raumfunktion in ägyptischen Tempeln des Neuen Reiches, MÄS, 2, Berlin, 1962.

AUBERT J.-F., AUBERT L., Statuettes égyptiennes. Chaouabtis, Ouchebtis, Paris, 1974, p. 27-74.

BAKRY H. S. K., The discovery of a temple of Sobk in Upper Egypt, MDAIK, 27,$_2$ 1971, p. 131-146.

BARGUET P., Le Livre des Morts des anciens Egyptiens, Paris, 1967.

——, Le temple d'Amon-Rê à Karnak. Essai d' exégèse, RAPH 21, Le Caire, 1962.

BARGUET P., DEWACHTER M., Le temple d'Amada. Cahier II. Description archéologique. Planches, Le Caire, 1967.

BAUD M., Les dessins ébauchés de la nécropole thébaine (au temps du Nouvel Empire), MIFAO 63, Le Caire, 1935.

BISSING F. W. VON, Denkmäler ägyptischer Sculptur, 3 vls., München, 1914.

BONNET H., Bilderatlas zur Religionsgeschichte, hrsg. v. H. Haas, 2-4. Lief.: Ägyptische Religion, Leipzig, 1924.

——, Reallexikon der ägyptischen Religionsgeschichte, Berlin, 1952.

BOTHMER B. V., More statues of Senenmut, BMA, 11, part 2, 1969-1970, p. 125-143.

BOUSSAC H., Tombeaux Thébains, Le tombeau d'Anna, MMAF 18, Paris 1896.

BRACK A., BRACK A., Das Grab des Haremheb, Theben Nr. 78, AV 35, Mainz, 1980.

——, ——, Das Grab des Tjanuni. Theben Nr. 74, AV 19, Mainz, 1977.

BREASTED J. H., Second preliminary report of the Egyptian expedition, AJSL, 25, 1908, p. 83-96.

BROVARSKI E., An allegory of death, JEA, 63, 1977, p. 178.

BRUNNER H., Die Geburt des Gottkönigs. Studien zur Überlieferung eines altägyptischen Mythos, ÄA 10, Wiesbaden, 1964.

——, Die südlichen Räume des Tempels von Luxor, AV 18, Mainz, 1977.

BRUNNER-TRAUT E., Gravidenflasche. Das Salben des Mutterleibes, Fs Galling, Tübingen, 1970, p. 35-48.

————, Das Muttermilchkrüglein. Ammen mit Stillumhang und Mondamulett, WdO, 5, 1969-1970, Göttingen, p. 145-164.

————, Nachlese zu zwei Arzneigefäßen, WdO, 6, 1971, Göttingen, p. 2-6.

————, Der Tanz im Alten Ägypten, ÄF 6, Glückstadt, 1938.

BRUYÈRE B., Deir el Médineh, Année 1926. Sondage au temple funéraire de Thotmès II (Hat Ankh Shesept), FIFAO 4, Le Caire, 1952.

————, Mert Seger à Deir El Médineh, MIFAO 58, Le Caire, 1930, p. 216-220, 250-1.

BUCHER P., Les Textes des tombes de Thoutmosis III et d'Aménophis II, MIFAO 60, Le Caire, 1932.

CAMINOS R. A., The New-Kingdom Temples of Buhen, ASE 33-4, 2 vls., London, 1974.

————, The Shrines and Rock-Inscriptions of Ibrim, ASE 32, London, 1968.

CAMINOS R. A., JAMES T. G., Gebel Es-Silsilah, ASE 31, London, 1963.

CARTER H., NEWBERRY P. E., The Tomb of Thoutmôsis IV (CG 46001-46529), London, 1904.

COONEY J. D., Gods bearing gifts for the King, The Bulletin of the Cleveland Museum of Art, November 1967, p. 279-289.

CORTEGGIANI J.-P., L'Egypte des pharaons au Musée du Caire, Paris, 1979.

CURTO S., Nubia, storia di una civiltà favolosa, Novara, 1965.

DARESSY G., Cercueils des cachettes royales (CG 61001-61044), Le Caire, 1909.

——, Fouilles de la Vallée des Rois (1898-1899) (CG 24001-24990), Le Caire, 1902.

——, Statues de divinités (CG 38001-39384), 2 vls., Le Caire, 1905-1906.

DAVIES N. DE G., Five Theban Tombs (being those of Mentuherkhepeshef, User, Daga, Nehemawäy and
     Tati), ASE 21, London, 1913.
——, The Tomb of Ḳen-Amūn at Thebes, 2 vls., PMMA 5, New York, 1930.
——, The Tomb of Nakht at Thebes, RPTMS 1, New York, 1917.
——, The Tomb of Puyemrê at Thebes, RPTMS 2-3, 2 vls., New York, 1922-1923.
——, The Tomb of Rekh-mi-Rē^c at Thebes, PMMA, 11, 2 vls., New York, 1943.
——, The Tomb of Tetaky at Thebes (N° 15), JEA, XI, 1925, p. 10-18.
——, The Tomb of Two Sculptors at Thebes, RPTMS 4, New York, 1925.
——, The Tombs of Two Officials of Thutmosis the Fourth (Nos 75 and 90), TTS 3, London, 1923.
——, The Tombs of Menkheperrasonb, Amenmosě, and another, (Nos 86, 112, 42, 226), TTS, 5, London,
     1933.
DAVIES N. DE G., GARDINER A. H., The Tomb of Amenemhēt (N° 82), TTS 1, London, 1915.
DAVIS T., NAVILLE E., The Tomb of Hâtshopsîtû, London, 1906.
DESROCHES-NOBLECOURT CH., Les religions égyptiennes, in "Histoire générale des religions", Paris, 1948, p.
     205-327.
DESROCHES-NOBLECOURT CH., DONADONI S., MOUKHTAR G., Le Speos d'El-Lessiya. Cahier I. Description
     archéologique. Planches, Le Caire, 1968.
DRIOTON E., Deux cryptogrammes de Senenmout, ASAE, 38, 1938, p. 231-246.
DUNHAM D., JANSSEN J.M.A., excavated by G. A. REISNER, Second Cataract Forts, vol. I. Semna-Kumma,
     Boston, 1960.
EGYPT's GOLDEN AGE; The Art of Living in the New Kingdom, 1558-1085 B.C., Catalogue of the Exhibition,
     Museum of Fine Arts Boston, February 3 – May 2 1982, Boston, 1982.
ENGELBACH R., Statues of the "soul of Nekhen" and the "soul of Pe" of the reign of Amenophis III, ASAE,
     42, 1943, p. 71-3.
THE EPIGRAPHIC SURVEY in cooperation with the Department of Antiquities of Egypt, The Tomb of Kheruef,
     Theban Tomb 192, Chicago, 1980.
ERMAN A., Die Religion der Ägypter. Ihr Werden und Vergehen in vier Jahrtausenden, Leipzig, 1934.
FAKHRY A., Tomb of Paser (N° 367 at Thebes), ASAE, 43, 1943, p. 389-414.
FARINA G., La pittura egiziana, Milano, 1929.
FOUCART G., Un temple flottant, le vaisseau d'or Amon-Râ, MonPiot, 25, 1921-22, p. 143-169.
——, La Belle fête de la Vallée, BIFAO, 24, 1924.
GAYET A., Le Temple de Louxor I: Constructions d'Aménophis III, MMAF, 15, Paris, 1894.
GOYON J.-C., Rituels funéraires de l'Ancienne Egyptě. Le Rituel de l'Embaumement; Le Ritual de l'Ouver-
     ture de la Bouche; Les Livres des Respirations, Paris, 1972.
GÖTTER, PHARAONEN. Katalog der Ausstellung, München, 1979.
GUKSCH H., Das Grab des Benja, gen. Paheqamen. Theben Nr. 343, AV 7, Mainz, 1978.
HABACHI L., Divinities adored in the area of Kalabsha, with a special reference to the goddess Miket,
     MDAIK, 24, 1969, p. 169-183.
HASSAN A., Stöcke und Stäbe im pharaonischen Ägypten bis zum Ende des Neuen Reiches, MÄS, 33,
     München-Berlin, 1976.
HAYES W. C., Royal Sarcophagi of the XVIII Dynasty, Princeton, 1935.
——, The Scepter of Egypt. A Background for the Study of the Egyptian Antiquities in the Metropolitan
     Museum of Art. Part II. The Hyksos Period and the New Kingdom (1675-1080 B.C), Cambridge 1959
     and (sec. ed.) New York, 1968, p. 43-279.
HELCK W., Das thebanische Grab 43, MDAIK, 17, 1961, p. 99-110.
HERMANN A., Die Stelen der thebanischen Felsgräber der 18. Dynastie, ÄF, 11, Glückstadt-Hamburg-New
     York, 1940.
HIRMER M., OTTO E., Ägyptische Kunst, Band 1., München, 1967, p. 208-281.
HORNUNG E., Ägyptische Unterweltsbücher, Zürich-München, 1972.
——, Das Amduat. Die Schrift des verborgenen Raumes, 3 vls., ÄA 7 (1,2), 13, Wiesbaden, 1963-67.
——. Das Buch der Anbetung des Re im Westen (Sonnenlitanei). Nach den Versionen des Neuen Reiches.
     Teil II: Übersetzung u. Kommentar, AH 3, Basel-Genève, 1977, p. 56-7.
——, Die Grabkammer des Vezirs User, NAWG, 1961, Nr. 5.
——, Das Totenbuch der Ägypter, Zürich-München, 1979.
HORNUNG E., STAEHELIN E., Studien zum Sedfest, AH, 1, Basel-Genève, 1974.
KARKOWSKI J., The Question of the Beautiful Feast of the Valley Representations in Hatshepsut's Temple at
     Deir el-Bahari. Acts, First International Congress of Egyptology, Cairo, October 2-10, 1976, edited by
     W. F. Reineke, Berlin, 1979, p. 359-364.
KEES H., Der Götterglaube im Alten Ägypten, sec. ed., Berlin, 1956.
——, Der Opfertanz des ägyptischen Königs, Leipzig, 1912.

KLEBS L., Die Reliefs und Malereien des Neuen Reiches (XVIII-XX. Dyn., ca 1580-1100), Material zur ägyptischen Kulturgeschichte, Teil I: Scenen aus dem Leben des Volkes, AHAW, 9, Heidelberg, 1934.

KRIÉGER P., Une statuette du roi-faucon au Musée du Louvre, RdE, 12, 1960, p. 37-58.

KUHLMANN K.P., Der Thron im Alten Ägypten. Untersuchungen zu Semantik, Ikonographie und Symbolik eines Herrschaftszeichens, ADAIK, Ägyptologische Reihe, 10, Glückstadt, 1977.

KÜHNERT-EGGEBRECHT E., Die Axt als Waffe und Werkzeug im alten Ägypten, MÄS, 15, Berlin, 1969.

LACAU P., Stèles de la XVIII Dynastie, Le Caire, 1957 (CG 34087-34189).

——, Stèles du Nouvel Empire, Tome I, fasc. 1 (1909), fasc. 2 (1926), Le Caire (CG 34001-34064 and 34065-34186).

LACAU P., CHEVRIER H., Une chapelle d'Hatshepsout à Karnak, 2 vls., I.-1977; II-1979, Le Caire.

LANGE K., HIRMER M., Aegypten, München, 1955, pl. 114-175; sec. ed. 1967, pl. 122-177.

LAUFFRAY J., Karnak d'Égypte. Domaine du divin, Paris, 1979.

LECLANT J., La fête Sed au temple jubilaire d'Aménophis III, Soleb (Soudan), Résumé des Cours et Travaux, Annuaire du Collège de France, 1979-80.

LEGRAIN G., Statues et statuettes de rois et de particuliers, I, Le Caire, 1906 (CG 42001-42138).

——, Les temples de Karnak, Bruxelles, 1929.

LEGRAIN G., NAVILLE E., L'aile nord du pylône d'Aménophis III à Karnak, Annales du Musée Guimet, 30, Paris, 1902.

LEPSIUS C. R., Denkmaeler aus Aegypten und Aethiopien, III, Berlin, pl. 1-90.

LETELLIER B., La cour à péristyle de Thoutmosis IV à Karnak (et la "cour des fêtes" de Thoutmosis II), "Hommages à la mémoire de Serge Sauneron", vol. I, Le Caire, 1979, p. 53-71.

——, La cour à péristyle de Thoutmosis IV à Karnak, BSFE, 84, mars 1979, p. 33-49.

LEXIKON DER ÄGYPTOLOGIE. Lieferungen 1-28, Wiesbaden, 1972-1981.

LIPIŃSKA J., The Temple of Tuthmosis III. Architecture (Deir El-Bahari II), Varsovie, 1977.

LORET V., La tombe de Khâ-m-hâ, MMAF, 1, Paris 1884, p. 113-133.

THE LUXOR MUSEUM OF ANCIENT EGYPTIAN ART . Catalogue, Cairo, 1979.

MACIVER D., WOOLEY L., Buhen, Philadelphia, 1911.

MANNICHE L., Ancient Egyptian Musical Instruments, MÄS, 34, München-Berlin, 1975.

MICHALOWSKI, K., Art of Ancient Egypt, New York, 1968.

MORENZ S., Gott und Mensch im alten Ägypten, Leipzig, 1964.

MORET, A., Du caractère religieux de la royauté pharaonique, Paris, 1902.

——, Le rituel du culte divin journalier en Egypte, Paris, 1902.

MUHAMMED M.A.-Qader, The Development of the Funerary Beliefs and Practices Displayed in the Private Tombs of the New Kingdom at Thebes, Cairo, 1966.

MÜLLER H.-W., Ägyptische Kunst, Frankfurt am Main, 1970.

MYŚLIWIEC K., Le portrait royal dans le bas-relief du Nouvel Empire, Varsovie, 1976.

NAVILLE E., The XIth Dynasty Temple at Deir El-Bahari, Part I, EEF, 28, London, 1907, p. 63-7 and pls. XXVII-XXXI.

——, The Funeral Papyrus of Jouiya, London, 1908.

——, The Temple of Deir El-Bahari, I-VI, EEF 12-14, 16, 19, 27, 29, London, 1895-1908.

NELSON H.H., Certain reliefs at Karnak and Medinet Habu and the ritual of Amenophis I, JNES, 8, 1949, p. 201-232.

——, The rite of "bringing the foot" as portrayed in Temple Reliefs, JEA, 35, 1949, p. 82-6.

NEWBERRY P.E., Scarab-shaped seals, London, 1907 (CG 36001-37521).

OTTO E., Das ägyptische Mundöffnungsritual, ÄA, 3; 2 vls., Wiesbaden, 1960.

NEUGEBAUER O., PARKER R.A., Egyptian Astronomical Texts, London, vol. I, 1960, pl. 24-5; vol. III, 1969, pl. 1-2.

PIANKOFF A., The Litany of Re, BS 40, 4, New York, 1964, p. 13-21.

PIANKOFF A., HORNUNG E., Das Grab Amenophis'III. im Westtal der Könige, MDAIK, 17, 1961, p. 111-127.

PORTER B., MOSS R.L.B., Topographical Bibliography of Ancient Egyptian Hieroglyphic Texts, Reliefs, and Paintings, 7 vls., Oxford, 1927-1952; sec. ed. vol. I – 1960, vol. II – 1972.

QUIBELL J. E., Tomb of Yuaa and Thuiu, Le Caire, 1908 (CG 51001-51191).

RADWAN A., Amenophis III dargestellt und angerufen als Osiris (Wnn-nfrw), MDAIK, $29_{,1}$ 1973, p. 71-6.

——, Die Darstellung des regierenden Königs und seiner Familienangehörigen in den Privatgräbern der 18. Dynastie, MÄS, 21, Berlin, 1969.

——, Zur bildlichen Gleichsetzung des ägyptischen Königs mit der Gottheit, MDAIK, $31_{,1}$ 1975, p. 99-108.

RÖSSLER-KÖHLER U., Zur Datierung des Falkenbildes von Hierakonpolis (CGC 14717), MDAIK, 34, 1978, p. 117-125.

SADEK A.-A.F., A Stela of Purification from the Tomb of Kha'emhat at Thebes, MDAIK, $29_{,1}$ p. 63-9.

SAYED R.el, Les sept vaches célestes, leur taureau et les quatre gouvernails, d'après les données de documents divers, MDAIK, 36, 1980, p. 357-390.

Säve-Söderbergh T., On Egyptian Representations of Hippopotamus Hunting as a Religious Motive, Uppsala, 1953.

——, Four Eighteenth Dynasty Tombs, PTT, 1, Oxford, 1957.

Schäfer H., Die "Vereinigung der Beiden Länder". Ursprung, Gehalt und Form eines ägyptischen Sinnbildes im Wandel der Geschichte, MDAIK, 12, 1943, p. 73-95.

Scharff A., Gott und König in Aegyptischen Gruppenplastiken, "Studi in Memoria di Ippolito Rosellini, vol. I, Pisa, 1949, p. 301-321.

Schiaparelli E., La tomba intatta dell' architetto Cha nella necropoli di Tebe (Relazione sui lavori della missione archeologica italiana in Egitto, anni 1903-1920), vol. II, Torino, 1927.

Schmidt V., Sarkofager, Mumiekister og Mumiehylstre i det Gamle AEgypten. Typologisk Atlas, København, 1919.

Schneider H.D., Shabtis. An Introduction to the History of Ancient Egyptian Funerary Statuettes, with a Catalogue of the Collection of Shabtis in the National Museum of Antiquities at Leiden, 3 vls., Leiden, 1977.

Schott S., Das Löschen von Fackeln in Milch, ZÄS, 73, 1937, p. 1-25.

——, Das schöne Fest vom Wüstentale, Festbräuche einer Totenstadt, AMAW, 11, Wiesbaden, 1953.

——, Die Reinigung Pharaohs in einem memphitischen Tempel (Berlin P 13242), NAWG, 1957, Nr. 3.

——, Zum Weltbild der Jenseitsführer des Neuen Reiches, "Göttinger Vorträge vom Ägyptologischen Kolloquium der Akademie am 25. und 26. August 1964", NAWG, 1965, Nr. 11, p. 185-197.

Seeber Ch., Untersuchungen zur Darstellung des Totengerichts im Alten Ägypten, MÄS, 35, München-Berlin, 1976.

Settgast J., Untersuchungen zu altägyptischen Bestattungsdarstellungen, ADAIK, Ägyptologische Reihe, 3, Glückstadt-Hamburg-New York, 1963.

Siclen III Ch. C. van, Two Theban Monuments from the Reign of Amenhotep II, San Antonio, Texas, 1982.

Simpson W.K., A Horus-of-Nekhen Statue of Amunhotpe III from Soleb, BMFA, 69, 1971, N° 358, p. 152-164.

Smith W.S., Ancient Egypt as represented in the Museum of Fine Arts, Boston, 1960.

Spiegel J., Die Entwicklung der Opferszenen in den Thebanischen Gräbern, MDAIK, 14, 1956, p. 190-207.

Steindorff G., Wolf W., Die Thebanische Gräberwelt, LÄS, 4, Glückstadt-Hamburg, 1936.

Strauss E.-Ch., Die Nunschale. Eine Gefäßgruppe des Neuen Reiches, MÄS, 30, München-Berlin, 1974.

Tylor J. J., Griffith F.LL., The Tomb of Paheri at El-Kab, EEF, 11, London, 1894.

——, Wall drawings and monuments of El Kab, The Tomb of Paheri, London, 1895.

Tylor J. J., Clarke S., Wall drawings and monuments of El Kab, The Temple of Amenhetep III, London, 1898.

Tylor J. J., Clarke, S., Griffith F.LL., Wall drawings and monuments of El Kab, The Tomb of Renni, London, 1900.

Valbelle D., Satis et Anoukis, Mainz, 1981, p. 112-121.

Vandier J., Manuel d'archéologie égyptienne, III, Les grandes époques, La statuaire, p. 291-331; IV, Bas-reliefs et peintures. Scènes de la vie quotidienne, Paris, 1964.

Vandier d'Abbadie J., La chapelle de Khâ, in "Deux tombes de Deir El-Médineh", MIFAO, 73, Le Caire, 1939, p. 1-18, pl. I-XVI.

Virey Ph., Sept tombeaux thébains de la XVIIIe dynastie, MMAF, 5, 2e fascicle, Paris, 1891.

Wallert I., Die Palmen im Alten Ägypten. Eine Untersuchung ihrer praktischen, symbolischen und religiösen Bedeutung, MÄS, 1, Berlin, 1962.

Walsem R. van, The psš-kf, An investigation of an ancient Egyptian funerary instrument, OMRO, 59-60, 1978-9, p. 193-248.

Wegner M., Stilentwicklung der thebanischen Beamtengräber, MDAIK, 4, 1933, p. 38-164.

Werbrouck M., Les pleureuses dans l'Egypte ancienne, Bruxelles, 1938.

——, Le Temple d'Hatshepsout à Deir El Bahari, Bruxelles, 1948.

Wildung D., Zwei Stelen aus Hatschepsuts Frühzeit, Festschrift zum 150-jährigen Bestehen des Berliner Ägyptischen Museums, Berlin, 1974, p. 255-268.

Wreszinski W., Atlas zur altägyptischen Kulturgeschichte, 3 vls., Leipzig, 1923-1936.

Zivie Ch.M., Giza au deuxième Millénaire, BdE, 70, Le Caire, 1976.

Source of Photographs

WALDEMAR JERKE: Pl. III, 2; XX, 1; XXI, 1; XLVI, 1.
JANUSZ KARKOWSKI: Pl. III, 3; XLV, 1.
KAROL MYŚLIWIEC: Pl. I, 2; II, 1; III, 1; IV, 1-4; V, 1; VI, 1-3; VII, 1-2; VIII, 1-2; IX, 1-3; X, 1-3; XIV, 1; XVII, 2; XIX, 1-2; XLV, 2.

I should like also to express my thanks to the following institutions for their invaluable contributions:
Centre Franco-Egyptien, Karnak: Pl. I, 1.
Deutsches Archäologisches Institut, Kairo (Photo. DIETER JOHANNES): Pl. XLVI, 2; XLVII, 1-2.
Fitzwilliam Museum, Cambridge: Pl. XXIII, 1.
Museo Egizio di Torino: Pl. XXIII, 2; XXXI, 2.
Metropolitan Museum of Art, New York: Pl. XXXIV, 2.

The titles of monographs, series and periodicals quoted in the "Introduction" and in the "Catalogue of Illustrations" are abbreviated according to the list published in the "Lexikon der Ägyptologie" I, Lieferung 8, p. XII-XXXIV. The complete form of these abbreviated titles which do not occur in that list is to be found in our "Bibliography".

INTRODUCTION

The victory of the Theban King Kamose over the Hyksos at the beginning of the 16th century B.C., and the unification of Lower and Upper Egypt after two centuries of partition (ca 1786-1570 B.C.) inaugurate a new chapter of Egyptian history.[1] Modern historians call it "the New Kingdom", and it comprises the Dynasties XVIII-XX (ca 1570-1085 B.C.). This long period may be divided into two phases, separated from each other by the so-called "religious revolution" of Amenophis IV-Akhenaten (ca 1379-1362 B.C.)—an episode of history which is also called "the Amarna Period". Almost every aspect of Egyptian culture, including religion, language and the arts, reveals considerable differences between the first and the second phases of the New Kingdom. The first one constitutes more or less a continuation of Middle Kingdom cultural traditions, whereas the second one displays many changes that were introduced at the end of the XVIIIth and the beginning of the XIXth Dynasties. The Amarna Period is therefore one of the most important turning-points of Egyptian history.

The subject of our study is the first phase of the New Kingdom, embracing two centuries, from the beginning of the XVIIIth Dynasty (ca 1570 B.C) up to the end of the reign of Amenophis III (ca 1379 B.C.). During this period Egypt developed into a great political and military power. The two first Kings of the Dynasty, Amosis (ca 1570-1546 B.C.) and Amenophis I (ca 1546-1526 B.C.) succeeded in restoring and strengthening Egypt within its legitimate borders. Amosis, the final conqueror of the Hyksos and the founder of the Dynasty, also had to cope with the usurper in Nubia and with some rebels in Upper Egypt. His successor was mainly preoccupied with Nubia. Amenophis I colonized Egypt's southern neighbour and a visible sign of this achievement was the function of Viceroy of Nubia, denominated by later pharaohs "the King's Son of Cush". We encounter this function for the first time in his reign. Amenophis I was the King whom Egyptians regarded as the creator of the country's might, and that is probably why a posthumous cult was dedicated to him at Thebes, lasting for several centuries, up to the Third Intermediate Period. Subsequent successors of Amenophis undertook many military campaigns to the South in order to put down insurrections in Cush, as well as to the Asiatic North-East, mainly to neighbouring Palestine. The greatest conquerors were Tuthmosis I (ca 1525-1512 B.C.), Tuthmosis III (ca 1504-1450 B.C.) and Amenophis II (ca 1450-1425 B.C.). The first of four Kings to bear the name "Tuthmosis" organized a military expedition to Mitanni, an Asiatic country situated beyond the Euphrates, and there took many prisoners. The only case for many centuries of an Egyptian army penetrating so far to the North-East was under the King's grandson Tuthmosis III. His victories over Palestine, Syria and Mitanni, as well as his expeditions to Nubia found artistic expression in some of the monumental scenes decorating Theban temples (Pl. XIX, 1). His son's, Amenophis'

---

[1] All chronological data in this fascicle are given according to the Cambridge Ancient History, Third edition, vol. II, part 2, Cambridge 1975, 1038.

II victorious campaigns (Pl. XIX, 2) seem to be the last important military achievements of the XVIIIth Dynasty. The monuments and inscriptions of Tuthmosis IV (ca 1425-1417 B.C.), and particularly those of his successor Amenophis III (ca 1417-1379 B.C.) have been witness to Egypt's greatest prosperity, although none of them recalls any great military success. During the long reign of Amenophis III the country has attained the zenith of its magnificence, which is also attested by the King's correspondence with Asiatic rulers.

A characteristic feature of the XVIIIth Dynasty monarchy was the distinguished role played by women, especially royal mothers, who were the recognized transmitters of sovereignty. The series of important and generally venerated queens starts with Tetisheri, the grandmother of Amosis, represented on this King's stela from Abydos (Pl. III, 2). She was the daughter of commoners, but she gave birth to both parents of Amosis. The King's wife, Aḥmose Nefertere had a special posthumous cult dedicated to her as mother of the great Amenophis I. She attained fame almost without parallel in the history of Egypt and she was often depicted together with her son, especially in tombs and on stelae of the Ramesside Period. Another famous queen was Aḥmose, the mother of Hatshepsut. She is represented several times in the temple at Deir el-Bahari (cf. Pl. III, 3). All these queen-mothers are iconographically characterized with a typical vulture-headdress, which stresses their association with the Queen- and Birth-Goddess Nekhbet, who was identified with this bird. The centre of her cult was at El-Kab where Amenophis III had dedicated a temple to her.[2]

None of these particular honors were endowed on the queen, nor subsequently the King Hatshepsut. Not only was she not venerated after her death, but also many of her reliefs and inscriptions were maliciously erased later on the orders of Tuthmosis III. The conflict between this King and his stepmother may be considered as the source of certain changes in the country's internal affairs or as the nucleus of an evolution, which ended a century later with the "religious revolution" of Amenophis IV. These political events were echoed in religious beliefs and practices. Important changes can be observed in the iconographic program of the Theban temples, and particularly the decoration of Theban tombs. Noticeable differences occurred between the period preceding the reign of Hatshepsut and the rule of her successors, until that of Amenophis III, whose monuments reveal particularities not attested before his reign.

Our knowledge of religious iconography of this period is for many reasons rather fragmentary. Almost all religious monuments of the XVIIIth Dynasty in Lower and Middle Egypt have been destroyed during the course of centuries. That is why our research must be limited to the reliefs and paintings which decorated the temples and tombs of Upper Egypt and Nubia. Theban monuments constitute our main source of information. The most important of the remaining Theban temples dating from this period are those at Karnak, Luxor and Deir el-Bahari. The last one, built in the time of Hatshepsut and partly decorated by her successor, is the only example of a Theban mortuary temple dating back to the XVIIIth Dynasty and surviving until our times.

A great number of these monuments is still unpublished. Only three temples have been recorded and publications issued about them in any almost satisfactory way: two temples

---

[2] Cf. Bibliography by TYLOR J. J., CLARKE S.; comp. PM, V, 188-9.

built by Hatshepsut—the "Chapelle Rouge" at Karnak (Pl. VII, 1; VIII, 1-2; IX, 1-3; X, 1-3; XIV, 1)[3] and her mortuary temple at Deir el-Bahari (Pl. XXXII, 1-2; XXXIII; XXXIV, 1)[4]—and parts of the Luxor temple of Amenophis III.[5] Among the unpublished ones still remain: at Karnak—all shrines built by Amenophis I, Tuthmosis I, Tuthmosis II, Amenophis II and Tuthmosis IV (Pl. II, 1; III, 1; IV, 1-4; V, 1; VI, 1-3; XVII, 2; XVIII, 1), the rooms of Hatshepsut (Pl. XI, 2; XII, 1-2), the following edifices by Tuthmosis III: his festival-hall (Pl. XI, 1; XIII, 1-2; XVI; XXII, 2; XXIV, 1), his granite sanctuary (Pl. XVII, 1), temple of Ptah (Pl. XIV, 2; XV, 1-2), the alabaster bark-station (Pl. VII, 2) and remains of some other buildings, as well as parts of temples built by Amenophis III in the North and in the South of Karnak; on the West side of Thebes—two important monuments of Tuthmosis III: his bark-shrine at Medinet Habu[6] and his temple erected at Deir el-Bahari, to the South of the Hatshepsut temple.[7] The latter one, discovered in 1961 and having material prepared for publication by the Polish Mission, offers particular interest for the study of iconography, the polychromy of its reliefs being well preserved. Since a great majority of temple reliefs have lost their painted details, the expected publication about this sanctuary may enrich our observations with some important points, which cannot be detected in other examples.

Besides the Teban sources, rich material four our study is provided by Nubian temples, most of them being already published. To the most important ones belong: the temple of Amūn-Rēᶜ and Rēᶜ-Ḥarakhti at Amada (temp. Tuthmosis III, Amenophis II and Tuthmosis IV),[8] the speos of Tuthmosis III at El-Lessiya, dedicated to the most important Nubian divinities,[9] the temples of Buhen, and particularly the one dedicated to Horus (temp. Tuthmosis III),[10] the temple built by Tuthmosis III for the Nubian god Dedwen and the deified King Sesostris III at Semna,[11] the temple erected by the same King for Khnum at Kumma[12] and the rock-chapels at Qasr Ibrim built in the time of Tuthmosis III and Amenophis II.[13] There remain still some important unpublished temples in Nubia, such as the temple built by Amenophis III at Soleb[14] or two temples on Elephantine: the one dedicated to Satis by Tuthmosis III[15] and the temple built for Khnum by Amenophis III.[16] A great deal of iconographic material is also preserved in one Upper Egyptian sanctuary, i.e. the temple of Nekhbet at El-Kab (temp. Amenophis III).[17]

---

[3] Cf. Bibliography by LACAU P., CHEVRIER H.

[4] Cf. Bibliography by NAVILLE E., The Temple of Deir el-Bahari.

[5] Cf. Bibliography by BRUNNER H., Die südlichen Räume; comp. PM, II, 316-333.

[6] PM, II, 466-472.

[7] Cf. Bibliography by LIPIŃSKA J.

[8] Cf. Bibliography by ACHIERY H. EL, BARGUET P., DEWACHTER M./Amada I/; BARGUET P., DEWACHTER M./Amada II/; ALY M., ABDEL-HAMID F., DEWACHTER M./Amada IV/.

[9] Cf. Bibliography by DESROCHES-NOBLECOURT CH., DONADONI S., MOUKHTAR G.

[10] Cf. Bibliography by CAMINOS R.A., The New Kingdom Temples.

[11] Cf. Bibliography by DUNHAM D., JANSSEN J.M.A.; comp. PM, VII, 145-9.

[12] PM, VII, 152-5.

[13] Cf. Bibliography by CAMINOS R.A., The Shrines.

[14] Cf. Bibliography by BREASTED J.H. and by LECLANT J.

[15] W. KAISER in MDAIK: 26 (1970), 109-111, pl. XLII; 27,₂ (1971), 195-6, pl. XLVIII; 28,₂ (1972), 158-161; 36 (1980), 250-264, pl. LVIII-LIX.

[16] Id. in MDAIK, 26, 1970, 111-3.

[17] Comp. note 2.

A great part of the reliefs which decorated these buildings has been destroyed. Their poor state of preservation is due to, among other things, the activity of later religious iconoclasts, especially those who lived in the time of Akhenaten, and to the restoration works done by his successors. On the other hand, the origin of numerous statues and fragmentary reliefs, which originally belonged to these buildings and are now distributed in different museums, is unknown. The situation is different with our second rich source of information, namely the Theban tombs of the nobles. The decoration of many tombs is well preserved. More than 150 tombs hewn in the rock at the edge of desert on the West bank of Thebes date back to the time between the reigns of Amosis and Amenophis III.[18] Their walls were sometimes decorated with bare paintings, sometimes with painted reliefs. Many reliefs have lost their original polychromy. There are preserved at El-Kab three other tombs of interest for iconographic studies,[19] and apart from their historical inscriptions their importance consists of their representing the early phase of the XVIIIth Dynasty tomb decoration—the period from Amosis to Tuthmosis III.

At this time the capital of Egyptian empire was Thebes (ancient Egyptian "Wast", modern Luxor), and its chief divinity, Amūn, became the first god of Egyptian pantheon. He was often associated with the solar god Rēᶜ and as such was venerated in numerous Theban temples. The main sanctuary of his cult was in Ipt-swt (modern Karnak), where subsequent Kings of the XVIIIth Dynasty enlarged the temple erected by the rulers of the Middle Kingdom and constructed new chapels within its precincts. This large "temenos" of Amūn-Rēᶜ was surrounded by temples dedicated to other important gods of the Theban pantheon. On its northern side there was the temple of Monthu, a god who was the predecessor of Amūn as chief divinity of the Theban nome. On the south side of the principal "temenos" there existed a temple dedicated to the goddess Mut, consort of Amūn and mother of Khons, who was the third member of the Theban triad. The precincts of Monthu and Mut contained temples built by various Kings, but the nucleus of their remaining parts belongs to the time of Amenophis III. Of similar date is also the oldest existing part of the Luxor temple, situated further southwards on the eastern bank of Thebes. This temple was called "Ipt rst" ("the southern harem") and was connected with the cult of "Amūn in the harem", an incarnation of this god associated with the ityphallic god Min. All these temples were places where a daily ritual was performed by priests, and where religious and political feasts were attended by common people.

The West of Thebes, situated on the other side of the Nile, was the domain of the dead. From the beginning of the XVIIIth Dynasty the Kings were buried in tombs hewn in the rock of the great pyramid-shaped mountain which overhangs a narrow valley, now called "the Valley of the Kings". An integral part of every royal sepulchre was the mortuary temple built at the edge of cultivated fields, several kilometers eastwards from the Valley. Only one of the XVIIIth Dynasty mortuary temples has survived in good condition to our times. This is the temple of Hatshepsut at Deir el-Bahari. Of another monumental temple, built at the edge of the Theban necropolis for Amenophis III, all that remains are the two colossal statues representing the King, the so-called "colossi of Memnon" (Pl. XLV, 2). All other mortuary temples of this time are destroyed right down to their foundations.

---

[18] PM, I,$_1$, passim.

[19] Cf. Bibliography by TYLOR J. J., GRIFFITH F. Ll.; TYLOR J. J., CLARKE S., GRIFFITH F. Ll; comp. PM, V, 177-181, 182-3.

Some other shrines and chapels were built in the vicinity of Theban necropolis. One of them is the bark-station of Tuthmosis III at Medinet Habu,[20] another one was the above-mentioned sanctuary built by the same King at Deir el-Bahari. The religious function of the latter has so far remained unclear. Behind these temples, in the rocky hills at the edge of the desert the necropolis of the nobles was situated. There hundreds of decorated tombs have survived until our days.

Although mortuary temples were built for the cult of the chief Theban gods and of the deceased King, the West of Thebes is mainly connected with gods of the other world. To the gods who were particularly venerated there belong Osiris, Anubis, Ḥathor, Western goddess, Termuthis, Wert-ḥekau and numerous divinities associated with the cult of Osiris. Another important dweller of the mythological world of the dead was the Sun-God in his various iconographic forms (cf. Pl. XXV, 2; XXVI, 2; XXVIII, 2; XXIX, 1-2; XXX).

Due to the scarcity of preserved material, we can hardly say anything about iconographic aspects of beliefs and rituals in the northern parts of Egypt at this time. Since almost no relics from the XVIIIth Dynasty have been preserved in Heliopolis, Memphis or Abydos, we only can observe the chief gods of these important religious centres (such as Atum, Ptah or Osiris) as guests depicted in Theban temples and tombs.

The topography of the different cults and local iconographic particularities of the different gods can much better be observed in Nubia, where such divinities predominated as Satis, Anukis, Ḥathor, Isis, Nekhbet, Miket, Dedwen, Khnum, Horus, Amūn, Rēᶜ-Harakhti, Min and the deified King Sesostris III. The cult of the last, a King who conquered Nubia as far as the third Nile cataract, was probably established in Nubia by Tuthmosis III, who is depicted together with Sesostris III in some ritual scenes decorating the temples of Semna,[21] Kumma[22] and Buhen,[23] as well as the rock-chapels of El-Lessiya[24] and Gebel-Dosha.[25] Quite significant for the relationship between the deified and the living King is a scene at Buhen, where Tuthmosis receives the sign of life from Sesostris.[26] Among iconographic particularities of the Egyptian divinities depicted in Nubian temples, the scorpion decorating the head of Isis deserves our special attention. Such pictures of the goddess occur in the temples of El-Lessiya, Amada, Dakka, and Buhen.[27] We may presume that in Nubia Isis was already associated with the scorpion-goddess Selkis at the time of the XVIIIth Dynasty, this affinity being attested in Egypt by later iconographic sources.[28] Since Nubia always remained under the strong religious influence of Thebes, there was always an important place reserved for Amūn in Nubian temples.

---

[20] Comp. note 6.
[21] PM, VII, 149.
[22] PM, VII, 153-4.
[23] PM, VII, 135, 22 N.
[24] PM, VII, 90.
[25] PM, VII, 167.
[26] CAMINOS, The New Kingdom Temples of Buhen, I, pl. 91, similar scene at Kumma; DUNHAM-JANSSEN, Semna-Kumna, pl. 58.
[27] CAMINOS, op. cit., 54, note 3, pl. 64, 73; DESROCHES-NOBLECOURT and others, Le spéos d'El-Lessiya, I, 11 /D 8/; cf. J.-C. GOYON, Hededyt: Isis-scorpion et Isis au scorpion. En marge du papyrus de Brooklyn 47.218.50-III, BIFAO, 78(2), 440-442.
[28] LÄ, III, 189, particularly notes 29 and 47.

The functions of an Egyptian temple were manifold. It was the dwelling-house of the god's statue; it was a miniature picture of the world; it played the role of a centre of creation, and this was a centre for the cult of the god.[29] The temple was the meeting-place for the King with the god, and—much more frequently—a place where the priest was in contact with the god's statue. There were temples of different kinds. Besides the standard sanctuaries dedicated to the chief gods of local pantheons and to guest-divinities, built all over the country, temples of particular functions were erected in Thebes. Probably every Pharaoh commemorated his "sed"- jubilee with a festival temple. We do not know all of these buildings. Some of them have been destroyed in later times and their blocks reused as building material. Every king of the XVIIIth Dynasty erected his mortuary temple to the West of Thebes. There were chapels for the cult of the King's parents and for the principal gods of the Theban pantheon in these buildings. An important part of these temples' precinct or just a room in the temple itself was the King's symbolical palace. As has already been stated, the only remaining mortuary temple of the XVIIIth Dynasty is that of Hatshepsut at Deir el-Bahari. Its architectural structure and its decoration point to particular cults of two divinities in this part of the Theban necropololis: Ḥathor and Anubis. To these divinities separate parts of the building were dedicated: the chapels of Anubis situated at its northern side,[30] and a shrine of Ḥathor (Pl. XXXII, 1-2; XXXIII; XXX-IV, 1) bordering the temple to the South. Besides their eschatological character and funeral functions, the mortuary temples played the part of barge-stations, where the holy barge with the statue of a god was deposited for a short time during the "Feast of the Valley". For the same purpose separate buildings were also built on both sides of the Nile. They could either have had the architectural shape of a typical New Kingdom temple (like the building of Tuthmosis III at Medinet Habu) or been merely a kiosk consisting of one single room, e.g. the barge-stations of Amenophis I (Pl. VI) and Tuthmosis III (Pl. VII, 2). In these buildings were deposited divine barges during the "feast of Opet" (eastern bank of the Nile) or the "feast of the Valley" (western bank).

A typical New Kingdom temple comprised several parts with definite function and decoration. Its rear part was composed of many rooms which were accessible only to the priests. In these rooms the daily ritual was performed. The sanctuary was a room containing the cult statue of a god. The walls of this room were decorated with reliefs depicting the daily ritual and the liturgy of offerings. A special room was reserved for the divine barge which stood there on a socle. The function of this place can be compared to that of the throne-room in a palace. The scheme of this room's relief decoration may have its prototype in the above-mentioned barge-station of Amenophis I, which had been partially decorated by Tuthmosis I (Pl. VI), or may be the copy of a non-preserved Middle Kingdom pattern. On both the longer walls of this room analogous or similar scenes occur, depicting a barge, in front of which the King performs various rites. Arranged in one or two registers, the decoration of this room represents episodes of different rituals, e.g. the introduction of the ruler performed by a divinity, offering-rites (including scenes with offering-tables, comp. Pl. X, 1), a god embracing a Pharaoh, scenes of daily ritual showing a King libating, making an offering or burning incense before a god, procession-scenes

---

[29] ARNOLD, Wandrelief, 3.
[30] PM, II, 353-6, 362-3. A new publication on both chapels of Anubis is being prepared by M. Witkowski.

etc. This variety of items leads one to conclude that there was no particular "ritual of the barge", but that all rites possible may have been performed at this place.

The room preceding the sanctuary contained an offering-table. From an architectural viewpoint it constitutes a passage between the rear parts of the temple and the frontal ones. That is why this room is sometimes denominated a "vestibule" or "pronaos". According to its ritual function, D. Arnold has proposed to call it "the room of the offering-table".[31] The relief decoration of this room consists of many offering-scenes. They represent a King offering such items as bread, salad, milk, wine, flowers, a figure of the goddess Ma^{c}et etc., to a god. The main tableau in this room shows the ruler consecrating an offering-table with a gesture of his hand. These scenes do not depict episodes of a particular ritual, but are a multiplied illustration of the room's function. The reliefs decorating this room in some temples show processions of offering-bearers transporting boxes with precious objects, which means that not only the daily meal, but also various gifts for gods could have been deposited in this part of the temple. There were also statues of Pharaohs or double statues representing a King with a god placed by the walls of "rooms of the offering-table". Two statues representing Amūn with a King (once Tuthmosis III and once Amenophis II) decorated one of such rooms in the temple of Karnak.[32] Fragments of them are still preserved in situ. On the walls of this room various ritual scenes may also have occurred, cf. that of "striking a ball" (Pl. XXXIII), showing the collar "menit" (Pl. XXXIV, 1), offering four boxes with cloths (Pl. X, 3; XI, 1), a god embracing a King (Pl. XV, 2), a King consecrating victims (pl. VII, 1-2) or bringing natron (Pl. XV, 1); a goddess suckling a King, Nile-gods bringing offerings (Pl. XLV, 1, 3), personifications of Lower and Upper Egypt (e.g. in the temple of Khnum at Kumma) or male and female personifications of Fertility bringing water (festival-temple of Tuthmosis III at Karnak), the scene of driving four calves (Pl. VI, 1), the Ennead of gods, the royal route with two vases (Pl. VIII, 1) or with an oar (Pl. VI, b) etc.

Several of the rooms in temples dedicated to gods were reserved for the cult of Kings. Such was the function of a) the chapel of purification, b) the chapel of the royal statue, and c) offering-rooms. These three types of rooms cannot always be clearly distinguished from each other, for each of them contains a similar scene showing a King seated on throne before an offering-table and receiving offerings from Thoth, Inmutf or from another King. With their decoration the "chapels of purification" commemorated the enthronement ritual. A series of scenes depicting this ceremony comprises such episodes as the purification of the King by Horus and Seth or Thoth, the introduction of the Pharaoh to the temple's chief divinity by two other gods (mainly Atum and Monthu or Khons), the fixing of a crown on the King's head by two gods, an offering-table scene, the coronation of the King performed by the chief god and some other rites. It is only exceptionally that these scenes constitute a continuous sequence decorating a wall. Separate tableaux of this cycle occur both in "chapels of purification" and in other rooms of each temple. The purification scene is, however, a constant iconograhic pattern in these chapels.[33] The "chapels of purification" were small rooms in which priests repeated some acts resembling those of

---

[31] ARNOLD, Wandrelief, 42.
[32] BARGUET, Temple d'Amon-Rê, 144, pl. XIV /D/; cf. PM, II, 105 (317), (318).
[33] ARNOLD, Wandrelief, 73.

the coronation cycle. A priest was, for example, purified and dressed in this room. His preparations for the ritual were then identified with the King's enthronement ceremonies.

A particular room, situated in the front part of a temple and connected with its pillared hall or its vestibule, was predestined for the cult of the royal statue. Besides the usual offering-table scene, the decoration of this room may contain chosen episodes from the daily ritual, as can be observed in the cult chapel of Tuthmosis I at Deir el-Bahari. The theme of funerary meal has problably been taken from the iconographic repertory of tomb reliefs. Other scenes characteristic for these rooms show the King making an offering to his predecessors and the unification of both parts of Egypt at the foot of his throne. This cult of Kings, which was connected with rooms of the royal statue, must be clearly distinguished from the cult of the rare deified pharaohs, who enjoyed a particular posthumous veneration, e.g. Amenophis I in Thebes or Sesostris III in Nubia. These Kings were honoured the same way as other gods and were supposed to have had the same magical power, whereas the royal statue in the rooms concerned was venerated as such, not as picture of a god. Royal statues of smaller size stood also in other parts of the temples, usually inside wall niches that were located in places predestined for bringing offerings or performing rites. Similar aspects of the royal cult are attested by scenes on votive stelae, showing e.g. Sesostris I and Tuthmosis III as equal counterparts in a symmetrically constructed scene (P. XXIII, 1) or an offering-bearer standing at an offering-table before a statue of Tuthmosis II (Pl. XXIII, 2).

A special room for funeral offering, belonging to the cult of the deceased King, existed in Theban mortuary temples. This should be considered as a transposition of similar rooms in Egyptian tombs. In the mortuary temple of Hatshepsut, one room of this kind is reserved for the cult of the Queen, and another one for that of Tuthmosis I. Each of them has a false-door stela in its western wall, and the longer walls of both of them are decorated with scenes showing the deceased at an offering-table.

An average temple has also several side-rooms of definite functions in the ritual. There are rooms for annointing and dressing, treasuries and slaughterhouses. Rooms for annointing and dressing are decorated with friezes of objects belonging to their ritual outfit. This pattern has been adopted from the decoration of earlier tombs and coffins. On the back wall of these rooms, there usually occurs a scene, in which the King uses one of the objects depicted in the frieze. Large scenes on their side-walls show the ruler offering the whole contents of a store to the temple's principal deity. A similar decoration scheme may be observed on walls of a treasury, i.e. a room in which precious ritual instruments were deposited. The reliefs on its longer walls show the King consecrating the ritual outfit, and the back wall scene again represents the monarch using one of these objects. The walls of the treasury in the festival-temple of Tuthmosis III at Karnak preserve rare scenes in which the King is shooting in the company of the god Seth—probably episodes of coronation or jubilee feasts.[34] The rite of consecrating slaughtered animals (Pl. VII) being a frequent item among scenes occurring in so-called ''slaughterhouses'', these rooms' function could have been as much practical as religious. Killing animals was part of rituals symbolizing the King's victory over his enemies. Other reliefs on the walls of ''slaughterhouses'' comprise scenes of offering food to gods.

---

[34] Id. Ib., 83; cf. LD, III, pl. 36 b.

The frontal parts of each temple were predestined for religious feasts. The "room of appearances" was a large pillared hall, a place where the god's boat-shrine containing his statue was emerging from the interior of its abode in order to appear to the public. The pillared hall constituted a procession way for the divine barge. Reviewed in this room's relief decoration are all the most important rituals and the feasts, which ever took place in the temple, including various episodes of the coronation cycle, processions of the barge, foundation ceremonies etc. Their aim is to commemorate the temple's history and to demonstrate its present life. There sometimes occur original scenes of royal propaganda showing e.g. the Ḥathor-cow licking a hand of Hatshepsut (Pl. XXXII, 1) or a King sitting between two goddesses.[35] In festival-temples or shrines of similar function, all faces of pillars in this room are decorated with standard scenes, in which a god greets or embraces the King and often gives him the sign of life (cf. Pl. XVII, 2).

"The room of appearances" gives into a large court called by Egyptians "the wide festival place". Its rear part constituted the temple's façade, often in the form of a monumental pylon. The front wall of the temple was usually decorated with large scenes of royal propaganda. A common motif at this place is the King receiving his insignia from the temple's chief god or offering to this god a figure of the goddess Maᶜet. This tableau gave to the public all important information about the temple: who its god was, who the temple's founder was, and which relationship existed between both of them. The King's victory over his enemies is another popular iconographic pattern in this place (Pl. XIX, 1-2). A monumental tableau of this kind could have an apothropaic meaning on a pylon, for the gate and the court were places that separated the divine cosmos from the terrestrial chaos.

Reliefs on the walls surrounding the court give some idea about feasts and ceremonies, which took place in the temple's open parts. They represent various episodes of the Opet-festival or those of the Valley-feast. Probably both of these festivals were depicted on the frontal wall of the upper terrace in the Deir el-Bahari temple of Hatshepsut.[36] There are also scenes from the coronation or from the "sed"-feast cycle on the walls of these open courts. The "sed"-feast is illustrated on the pylon of Amenophis III at Soleb.[37] In the temple of Amada, where the pillared hall also functioned as the court, there occurs one of the earliest versions of the scene with the "ished"-tree, belonging to a mythicized coronation or jubilee ritual.[38] The lower part of these walls often bears a frieze of Nile-god figures bringing offerings and thus personifying provinces of Egypt (Pl. XLV, 3), as well as processions of priests and cattle.

Some general rules may be observed in the relief decoration of Egyptian temples. The scenes decorating both side-walls of their rooms are dynamic in character, for they show the King or the priest walking in the direction of the sanctuary, the divinity being orientated in the opposite direction, as if it were stepping out of the temple. It is among the reliefs on these walls that one can often find individual iconographic solutions of some traditional patterns. The majority of scenes occurring on transversal walls has a more

---

[35] In Buhen: MACIVER D., WOOLEY L., Buhen, 50-6, pl. XIX-XX.

[36] Cf. Bibliography by KARKOWSKI, 359.

[37] Cf. Bibliography by BREASTED; comp. LD, III, pl. 83-6.

[38] ACHIERY H. EL and others, Amada I, pl. XXXII, fig. 30; BARGUET P., DEWACHTER M., Amada II, pl. XV-XVIII.

static expression caused by their didactic function. Their form is usually more traditional than in the case of reliefs on the side-walls.

A striking feature of Egyptian theology is its connection with the King's policy. That is why the ritual and its pictorial record are overwhelmed with political propaganda, visible in all reliefs decorating the temples. All scenes show the King in the company of various gods. Some of them represent actual episodes of these rituals, in which the King participated himself. But many of them must be interpreted as merely symbolical, conventionalised pictures of reality. The border between fact and artistic convention is not always clearly discernible. In many cases the King did not perform the rite in which he is depicted, but was represented by a priest—which does not occur on the picture. This certainly was the case for the daily ritual performed in all temples by priests.

All scenes of religious content may be divided in two categories: a) scenes showing actual rites and rituals, b) symbolical scenes either commemorating historical facts or mythicizing some ideas of theological and political propaganda. The second category doubtless incorporates several iconographic elements of real ceremonies.

A typical example of historical fact which was mythicised and represented in a cycle of tableaux is the "miraculous birth of the King". Two copies of this iconographic pattern have survived until now in Theban temples of the period concerned in this treatise.[39] The earlier one decorates a portico in the Deir el-Bahari temple of Hatshepsut,[40] and the later one occurs in the temple of Amenophis III at Luxor.[40] Each of them is composed of 15 episodes depicting the nativity cycle from the moment when the King of the gods, Amūn-Rēᶜ, decides to create a new King. The act of creation occurs in the presence of the goddesses Hemset and Selkis. The god plays the role of Hatshepsut's father, her mother being the Queen Aḥmosi (Deir el-Bahari). The divine father and a human mother are also represented as Amenophis' III parents (Luxor). In one of the following scenes Khnum is moulding the King's body on a potter's wheel. The child's birth, nourishment and circumcision are followed by scenes in which the King is accepted by Amūn and acclaimed by other gods. Amūn-Rēᶜ playing the role of the Queen's masculine counterpart, the King receives both a divine and a human nature. Being a real heir of the gods, he becomes a mediator between them and the people. Such a version of theogamy must be interpreted as a product of the XVIIIth Dynasty political theology.

A characteristic iconographic feature of the royal theogamy cycle is a reduplication of the child. One of two analogous figures shows the King himself, whilst his double represents the royal "Ka". The latter wears a standard with the King's Horus name. A similar figure accompanies the Pharaoh in many ritual scenes showing him before a divinity (cf. Pl. VI, 1; XIV, 2). More frequently this anthropomorphic figure is replaced by a "Ka"-standard provided with two human arms holding the sign of life, the feather symbolizing the truth (or justice) and the standard crowned with a royal head (cf. Pl. X, 1; XI, 1-2; XIII, 1). Another motif of the nativity cycle, that of suckling the royal child, occurs in the decoration of Theban tombs. The suckling goddess there is Termuthis, the lady of the granary (Pl. XXXV, 2), and the scene is usually associated with the harvest festival. It may therefore refer to a rite, which was performed at this occasion.

---

[39] PM, II, 347-8.
[40] GAYET, Temple de Louxor, pl. LXIII-LXVII; BRUNNER, Geburt des Gottkönigs, passim.

Many representations of the King in the tombs of Theban nobles illustrate another aspect of the general idea expressed through the cycle of royal theogamy. Being of both human and divine nature, the King plays the role of mediator between gods and people. That is why he is sometimes shown as receiving offerings from the deceased and his family, and sometimes as giving similar offerings to the gods. According to a reliable interpretation proposed by A. Radwan, this is a pictorial illustration of the popular formula "the offering that the King gives" which repeatedly occurs in funeral texts.[41] The Pharaoh makes an offering to a divinity for the deceased's sake, in order to gain the god's favour for him.

Ritual scenes in Egyptian temples are of two different kinds. Many of them represent subsequent episodes of *the daily ritual*, which was performed in the sanctuary by a priest. Other scenes show the ceremonies of *feasts and festivals*, which took place inside and outside the temple. Their principal officiant was the King. During the daily ritual the priest performed rites before the statue of the god. The statue remained in its permanent place and the ceremony was not accessible to the public. The feasts consisted in taking the god's boat-shrine out of the sanctuary and transporting it in procession from one temple to another. These ceremonies were attended by the King, the priests and large crowds of people.

The reliefs showing the daily ritual refer to a) the daily ritual of the cult-statue and b) the liturgy of offerings. The priest in charge of the daily ritual entered the sanctuary, opened the shrine containing the statue, prostrated himself in front of it, purified the statue with water, burned incense in front of it, dressed the statue with cloths, crowns and collars, and finished its toilet with the application of ointments and make-up. The god being washed, dressed and painted, the priest left the sanctuary and removed traces of his foot prints, so that no impurity remained in the god's abode. Scenes of this ritual usually occur on side-walls of the rooms for the cult-statue. The most frequently depicted episodes include the pouring of water on the god's statue out of the "nemset"- or "desheret"-jugs (Pl. XII, 1; XIII, 1-2), burning incense (Pl. XIII, 2; XIV, 2), bringing natron (Pl. XV, 1), touching the god (Pl. XII, 2), anointing and dressing him, bringing the foot, removing traces of foot steps from the floor and uncovering the god's face.[42]

The liturgy of offerings comprised such episodes as bringing the offering meal, bringing wine, milk, lettuce etc., presenting various offerings (Pl. IV, 1-4; Pl. XI, 1) and consecrating victims (Pl. VII, 1-2). There are also large offering-scenes on the rear walls of the "rooms for the cult-statue", but their meaning is only symbolical. They are not included in the "liturgy of offerings", but their function is to stress the general character of the temple as a place for offerings. Large offering-scenes, showing the most important moment of the liturgy, occur also in other rooms of Egyptian temples and they may refer to ceremonies, which actually took place there (cf. Pl. XI, 2).

The second kind of ritual scenes is connected with religious and political feasts. Egyptian feast calendars abound in days or longer periods dedicated to particular gods, commemorating some historical moments or connected with geographical phenomena. Among festivities of regal character the most important ones were organized on the occa-

---

[41] RADWAN, Darstellungen des regierenden Königs, 106.
[42] ARNOLD, Wandrelief, 9.

sion of the King's coronation and during his jubilee called "heb-sed" (the feast "sed"). The latter should have occurred on the 30th anniversary of a King's reign, but evidence from historical records proves that some rulers put forward the date of their first jubilee and celebrated more than one "sed"-festival at shorter intervals.

The coronation of the King belongs to the most popular items among Egyptian ritual scenes. The pictorial record of this historical moment has been standardized as a scene showing a kneeling King and a seated divinity (Pl. V, 2). This motif occurs in different parts of the temples and is constantly repeated on the pyramids crowning royal obelisks. A more developed version of the ceremony is represented in several scenes decorating the walls of the "Chapelle Rouge" (Hatshepsut) in Karnak.[43] In each of these scenes Amūn-Rē[c], seated behind the King, puts one hand on the ruler's crown and the other one on his shoulder. Both figures are represented as being inside a shrine, in front of which stands a goddess, different in every scene (Ḥathor, Mut, Ament etc.). She puts her left hand on the King's forehead and holds a "was" scepter in her right hand. The scepter is combined with the sign of life that the goddess brings up to the King's mouth. In every scene the Pharaoh is represented with a different crown, which may either have a merely symbolic meaning or may indicate that the rite was repeated several times. Another version of the coronation scene is attested on the wooden pannels which belonged to a throne of Tuthmosis IV (Pl. XXXIV, 2). A goddess (Wert-ḥekau in this case) standing before the Pharaoh brings her hand towards his crown, whereas Thoth, holding the pole of a hundred thousand years, stands behind the King. The latter is represented in the attitude of Osiris and with this god's insignia: a flagellum and a "ḥeka" sceptre. An original iconographic solution has been invented by the decorator of the Semna temple.[44] Tuthmosis III, crowned there by the temple's chief god Dedwen and introduced to him by Inmutf, kneels in front of a sophisticated figure, being a combination of various symbols: the god Ḥeḥ, a personification of the number "million", holds in each hand one pole of a hundred thousand years and supports a "was" scepter, to which is attached a sequence of three symbolic signs combined with two human hands directed towards the King's face.

The real course of the coronation ceremony can be reconstructed only fragmentarily on the base of some scenes dispersed in different temples. The aim of these representations was to show, that the chief divinity had chosen and all other gods have accepted as their heir a semi-human being. Therefore, in the temple of Hatshepsut at Deir el-Bahari the coronation cycle comprises both realistic and mythological scenes.[45] The royal child is first being introduced by Amūn to the gods of the South and the North, then purified by Horus and Amūn with water poured out of "ḥes" vases. As an adult ruler, the King is introduced by two gods to Atum, the chief divinity of the Lower Egyptian Heliopolis, and by the god Inmutf to Amūn. In the latter scene the King already wears the double crown of Lower and Upper Egypt as well as the insignia of his reign. Two divine secretaries, the goddess Seshat and the god Thoth, register this fact in the annals, and the gods representing both parts of Egypt jubilate at this event. Thereupon a terrestrial episode follows: the King is crowned by his real father in the presence of the Kingdom's high officers. Unlike

[43] LACAU-CHEVRIER, Chapelle, pl. II, III, XI.
[44] LD, III, pl. LIII.
[45] PM, II, 348-9 (II).

in the symbolical scenes, showing a kneeling Pharaoh crowned by a god, in this case the young King ist standing before his father. Separate scenes of this cycle, showing either the purification, the introduction, the registration in annals or on the pole of many years, sometimes additionally accompanied by the picture of a divinity making the "nini" purification with streams of water held in each hand (cf. Dedwen at Semna or Khnum at Kumma[46]) or else offering-scenes from this sequence became standard elements in the decoration of Egyptian temples (cf. Pl. XVII, 1). Some of these scenes, particularly in Nubian temples, are remarkable because of their original composition, revealing their authors' creative immagination. In the temple of Semna, e.g., Thoth is writing in annals together with the King himself, while the second divine secretary, the goddess Seshat, embraces the monarch.[47] The King holds in his other hand the pole of many years decorated with signs of life and stability, as if he had taken over this attribute from the gods. In a similar scene at Kumma the King is replaced by Khnum who in one hand holds a chain composed of signs symbolizing a great number of years, and in the other—the pole of a hundred thousand years. Thoth is writing on this pole and holding a bunch of similar signs in his other hand.[48] We may observe that the principle of symmetry observed by the decorator of both temples (Semna and Kumma) enables him to diversify the content of similar scenes according to the needs of local theologies. One may suppose that other rites also represented in the same sequence of scenes, such as so-called "ritual dances", consisting of the King's course with various ritual objects (PL. VI, 2; VIII, 1; X, 2) could have belonged to the coronation ritual.

An important rite of the coronation cycle is represented with a mythical scene of writing royal names on leaves of the "ished" tree. This rite originated probably in Heliopolis. The scene in the temple of Amada shows Tuthmosis IV crowned by Rēᶜ-Ḥarakhti-Atum, both of them appearing on a platform, which is supported by the lowest branch of the tree.[49] Thoth is writing on the pole of many years, and a neighbouring scene shows the young King being suckled by Ḥathor in the presence of gods Wert-ḥekau and Khnum. A later version of the scene with "ished" tree occurs in the Luxor temple of Amenophis III.[50] Amūn is writing the King's name on the leaves of the tree, and a parallel scene shows the same god putting his left hand on the ruler's double crown, whilst with his right hand he is bringing the symbols of life, rule and stability close to the King's mouth. The ceremony is attended by two goddesses holding poles of many years. One of them is wearing the crown of Upper Egypt, the other one is represented with the crown of Lower Egypt. This double-scene is situated over the entrance to one of the temple's rooms. Another version of the same scene is known from the temple of Tuthmosis III at Medinet Habu.[51] Two divinities, Atum and Ḥathor, lead the King to Amūn whose throne stands on a tall socle in front of the "ished" tree. It is Amūn, who is writing on the tree's leaves.

A rite, which probably took place after the coronation ceremony, was the King's shooting an arrow in each of the four cardinal directions of the world. This ceremony is

---

[46] LD, III, pl. 56, "a" and 58.
[47] LD, III, pl. 55, b.
[48] LD, III, pl. 59.
[49] BARGUET P., DEWACHTER M., Amada II, pl. XV, XVII; ALY M. and others, Amada IV, C 7.
[50] BRUNNER, Die südlichen Räume, pl. XIV, XLIX.
[51] LD, III, pl. 37, a.

represented in the Karnak festival temple of Tuthmosis III.[52] The King is drawing the string of his bow, while the god Seth embraces the monarch. This way the ruler is symbolically extending his power over the whole world. As an episode of the coronation ceremony may probably also be interpreted the rite of loosing four birds as heralds to announce the King's "appearing in glory". Tuthmosis III running with a bird towards Ḥatḥor is depicted once in Karnak[53] and once in his Kumma temple.[54] In both cases the King is holding several long scepters in his other hand and wearing the "atef" crown, whereas the goddess presents to him the "menit" necklace, a symbol of revival. With the same gesture the goddess Wert-ḥekau is represented standing before Amūn, who is described as granting the right of Hatshepsut to the throne (the shrine of Ḥatḥor in the Deir el-Bahari temple: Pl. XXXIV, 1). Juxtaposed with the scene in which the same goddess is crowning the King Tuthmosis IV (Pl. XXXIV, 2), this example illustrates the way of mythicizing episodes of actual rituals in the process of projecting iconographic patterns into the sphere of the dead, even in the case of several scenes being reminiscences of coronation and "sed" feast rituals.

As every Egyptian feast of importance, the coronation was probably connected with processions. Numerous representations of processions in Egyptian temples may include some impressions from the coronation festival. Such processions are usually composed of singers, dancers, musicians, offering-bearers, priests carrying statues or other ritual objects (cf. Pl. XXIV, 1) etc.

Some rites of the coronation cycle were presumably repeated at the King's jubilee, the feast "sed" being a confirmation of his office. Both festivals were preceded by the ritual of erecting a "djed"-pillar, a symbol of stability and renewal associated, among other meanings, with the victory of Osiris over his enemy. This fetish, composed of a pillar with some floral elements attached to it, was depicted as a pillar with horizontal platforms in its upper part. On one long wall in the Theban tomb of Kheruef (temp. Amenophis III) the ceremony of raising the "djed"-pillar is represented on the occasion of the King's "sed" feast.[55] The scene is composed of several pictures, showing first the act of raising the pillar, then a standing large-size fetish provided with human features that may suggest its identification with Osiris. The King and his wife are attending the ceremony on one side, and on the other there is a popular festival depicted with songs, dances and games. Subsequent scenes show processions of offering-bearers, singers, dancers and men jousting with papyrus-stalks (Pl. XLIV, 1-2).

Other rites of the "sed" festival are known from the reliefs decorating the temple of Amenophis III at Soleb.[56] These scenes being preserved but fragmentarily, our ideas about the course of the feast are far from being complete. An essential part of the ceremonies must have consisted of a procession around the city, including the rite of striking on the city gates.[57] Other episodes comprise the anointing of the throne, a procession with the figure of the god Wepwaut, rites in front of a shrine containing a statue of

[52] Comp. note 34.
[53] Barguet, Temple d'Amon-Rê, 120; cf. PM, II, 93 (267)-(268), II, 1.
[54] LD, III, pl. 57, b; Dunham-Janssen, Semna-Kumma, pl. 60.
[55] PM, I, 299, (7) The Epigraphic Survey, Chicago, pls. 47, 53-7.
[56] PM, VII, 170, (5)-(7).
[57] LD, III, pl. 83-6; cf. Bibliography by Breasted and Leclant.

Khnum, the ceremony of offering corn to the King, who transmits it to Khnum etc. All these rites were attended by the Pharaoh and his wife, and they extended over several days. A part of the "sed" feast must have been also the above-described shooting or four arrows, depicted in the festival-temple of Tuthmosis III at Karnak.[58] The culmination of the feast was the ceremony of dressing the King with a white coat and giving him the insignia of office— the "ḥeka" sceptre and a flagellum. Such are the features of every King in the standardized "sed" feast scene, which was reproduced in reliefs above monumental doors in numerous temples (cf. Pl. V, 1). The archtype of this iconographic pattern dates back to a period preceding the New Kingdom. It is conceived as a double-scene of antithetic composition. The King is seated in a kiosk and wears once the Lower Egyptian once the Upper Egyptian crown. This dualism of geographical and political background is projected on all elements of the scene. Two gods associated with both parts of the country offer to the monarch one or several poles of a hundred thousand years. These gods are usually Horus and Seth, depicted as animals standing on nome-standards which are provided with two human arms, one of them being extended towards the King and holding a pole. Various religious symbols surround the King and the gods. In the Karnak "sed" scene of Amenophis I (Pl. V, 1) there are, among others, two standards of Wepwaut on each side of the double-scene. Some standards are held by personified hieroglyphic signs "ankh" (life) and "was" (dominion). The gods of the South and the North are introduced in this case to the King by a goddess, Meret, standing on the sign of gold, and by Inmutf. The King usually appears in the attitude of Osiris, as a mummy shown in profile, with a flagellum in his hands. This association with the god of regeneration may stress the principal idea of the feast: the Pharaoh's reappearance as ruler of the entire country.

Another symbol of unification decorates the King's throne. This is the "sema-tawy", one of the most frequent motifs in Egyptian royal heraldry. It represents the plants of Lower and Upper Egypt, the papyrus and the sedge(?), bound at the "sema"-sign which is a combination of an animal lung and windpipe. Unnumbered versions of this symbol decorate different objects and their representations in Egyptian art. They belong to standard decoration of the royal throne, and often appear on frontal sides of altars and on the walls of Egyptian temples. The "sema"-symbol occurs as the central element in many decorative patterns of symmetrical composition. A relief of Tuthmosis I in Karnak (Pl. XVIII, 1) shows a cartouche of this King supported by the "sema"-symbol and accompanied by two lions raised upon nome-standards. Each lion has a falcon-head wearing a royal crown composed of horns and feathers. The most frequent version of this scene shows two Nile-gods as personifications of both parts of Egypt in the act of binding the symbolical plant around the "sema"-symbol. The attitude of Nile-figures and their attributes vary. They may be standing, stepping with one leg on their plants, and wearing clumps of symbolic plants on their heads (cf. reliefs of Amenophis III on the thrones of his colossal statues which belonged to his mortuary temple; Pl. XLV, 2) or be seated and accompanied by two lions (cf. as decoration of the socle supporting the throne in reliefs of Tuthmosis III at Karnak; Pl. XVIII, 2). The same idea of unification could also be expressed with other iconographic means, which may generally be reduced to the principle of symmetry and parallelism of scenes, gods and symbols. A large scene in the speos of

---

[58] Comp. note 34.

Tuthmosis III at El-Lessiya shows the King seated on a throne between Nekhbet, the god-dess of the South, and Wadjet—her northern counterpart.[59] On both sides of this central motif there are two scenes, one showing the King making an offering to a god and one of a god rewarding the monarch. Similar is the composition of a scene in the temple of Kum-ma, where the King, provided with insignia of his office, is seated between the gods Khnum and Sesostris III.[60] Khnum embraces the Pharaoh, and Sesostris gives him the sign of life. These scenes may be compared with a tableau from the ''sed''-feast cycle in the festival temple of Tuthmosis III at Karnak.[61] The King, wearing his double-crown and holding his insignia, is seated between two goddesses, each of them holding one pole of a hundred thousand years in each hand. The scene is bordered by the figures of two other goddesses provided each with one pole of many years. All attributes held by parallel figures of both pairs of divinities are disposed in accordance with the principle of sym-metry. This kind of composition occurs in the majority of scenes situated on the axis of a temple, e.g. on lintels and above them or on the sanctuaries' rear walls.

On the occasion of the ''sed'' feast the King rewarded his high officials with gifts and donated fields to the temples of principal gods. He commemorated his festival by erecting a new temple that we call ''festival-temple''. Such was the origin of the Soleb temple of Amenophis III[62] and of some buildings in Karnak, cf. those of Amenophis I (Pl. II, 1; III, 1; IV, 1-4), Amenophis II (Pl. XVII, 2) and Tuthmosis III (Pl. XI, 1; XIII, 1-2; XXII, 2; XXIV, 1). A typical feature of these temples is the pillared hall where the King is represented in multiple similar scenes showing him with a god, most frequently Amūn, who either embraces the Pharaoh and (or) gives him the sign of live (Pl. XVII, 2) or receives from him various offerings (Pl. IV). The garments of the King in these scenes, and particularly the great variety of his crowns, could be the subject of a separate work. No comprehensive study of their meaning and iconography has been done hitherto. Special attention should be paid to the complicated feather-crowns, which are composed of different horns, uraei and feathers arranged in many various ways (cf. Pl. I, 2; VI, 1; VII, 1; VIII, 2; X, 3; XI, 1-2; XVII, 2; XXI, 1; XXXII, 1; XXXIII, and similar crowns worn by Osiris, cf. Pl. XXXI, 1-2, and Sobk, cf. Pl. XLVII, 2). Crowns of this kind were worn by the King during other festivities as well, therefore the iconograpic material of the ''sed''-feast temples should be compared with that provided by all other reliefs and paint-ings. The aim of such a study should be to observe the connection between the King's crown or dress and the ritual in which it occurs.

All this symbolism stemming from the King's coronation, reign and jubilee returns also on the occasion of other feasts. The most commonly illustrated scenes of royal propaganda include the huge tableaux on the pylons of Egyptian temples. They represent the King smiting foreign captives before an Egyptian god (Pl. XIX, 1-2). Although some victory feasts, commemorating the actual military achievements of the Pharaohs, are attested by written sources (cf. a feast of Tuthmosis' III victory by Megiddo[63]), the scenes on the

---

[59] DESROCHES-NOBLECOURT and others, Le spéos d'El-Lessiya, I, pl. XIX; ACHIERY and others, Le spéos d'El-Lessiya, II, pl. XIII (D 13-17).

[60] LD, III, pl. 57, a; DUNHAM-JANSSEN, Semna-Kumma, pl. 58.

[61] Id. Ib., pl. 35, a.

[62] Comp. notes 56-7.

[63] LÄ, II, 183.

pylons should be interpreted as general symbols of the King's victory over his enemies. Their didactic character may be deduced from their dimensions and their occurring on the pylons' frontal walls, a place accessible to everybody at any time. This iconographic pattern was elaborated at early Dynastic times, and its prototype seems to be the picture on the palette of Narmer. In these scenes the King always holds a mace in one raised hand, whiles his other hand catches a pole, to which foreigners are bound by their hair. The ceremony is attended by Amūn represented in the scene's upper corner, within a square bordered with a frame, which seems to separate the historical event from the divine sphere. Particularly rich in details is the scene on the pylon of Tuthmosis III (Pl. XIX, 1). Underneath the god is represented a goddess introducing the so-called ring-names of foreign people, ranged in horizontal lines and filling a great part of the surrounding surface. Each of these figures is composed of a geographical name written inside an oval ring that is combined with the upper part of a foreigner's body. The hands of each captive are bound together behind his ring. Both the names and the faces of these figures characterize foreign nations, which had been conquered by the King. The ring-names became a popular decorative motif occurring not only on pylons, but also constituting the friezes which adorn the socle of the royal throne (cf. Pl. XX, 2). At this place they materialize the idea of ''putting foreign people under the King's foot''—a common phrase in the royal titulature. Some faces of these foreigners are rendered by Egyptian artists as portraits with real features of the people's physiognomy. Such is the case of the ring-names decorating the socle of Amenophis III represented in the tomb of Kheruef (Pl. XXI, 2).

A frequent item used as adornment for the royal throne is also the ''sema''-symbol of unification, to which two foreigners are attached, one of them representing the peoples of the North, and the other one—those of the South (cf. Pl. XX, 2). The usual propaganda concerning both parts of Egypt is here extended upon foreign peoples of both geographical orientations.

Another mythicized version of the King's victory is the popular scene showing a sphinx with King's head trampling foes (cf. Pl. XX, 2; XXI, 1). As can be deduced from a representation of the sphinx on the chariot found in the tomb of Tuthmosis IV (Pl. XXI, 1), this iconographic pattern was intended not only to express the Pharaoh's identity with the lion, but also stress his association with other gods. The animal's feathered skin is a feature of the falcon-god Horus, and the horn at the King's face should be interpreted as a reminiscence of the ram-headed Amūn. The King would then be trampling foes as a being of divine nature. Besides this mythicized version of the victory, there also occurs a realistic one on the same chariot of Tuthmosis IV (Pl. XX, 1). The detailed treatment of the King's military garment in this scene provides some important material for iconographic studies. We may observe that an association with Horus is in this scene also rendered by means of a feathered skin. The King's apron is made of such a material.

The motif of the King trampling foes did not only decorate such objects as thrones or chariots, but may also have been copied in larger size on the walls of a temple. One of the porticoes in the Deir el-Bahari temple of Hatshepsut provides an interesting example of associating this pattern with scenes of hunting and fowling.[64] Two monumental pictures showing the victorious royal sphinx in this case border the scenes concerned. As all these

---

[64] PM, II, 342, (7)-(9).

tableaux constitute one continuous series on the walls of this portico, the representations of
the King's hunting and fowling may be interpreted as metaphors of his victories.[65] The
same meaning has been suggested for a scene in Karnak, showing Tuthmosis III with a
hippopotamus.[66] This animal's association with the god Seth might support this
hypothesis, for the Pharaoh was identified with his enemy Horus. Several later copies of
this scene may point to a ritual with the hunt as its leit-motif.

Some ritual performances and probably also popular festivities took place at the occasion of the important event, which was the foundation of a new temple. The iconographic
repertory of Egyptian temple reliefs comprises several scenes giving an idea about these
rites. The King and the goddess Seshat fix the limits of a new temple—such is the item of a
standardized scene, which repeatedly occurs in temple reliefs of the XVIIIth Dynasty, e.g.
in the "Chapelle Rouge" of Hatshepsut (Pl. VIII, 2), among scenes of Tuthmosis III at
Amada[67] and in Karnak.[68] The King and the goddess, facing each other, are straining a
line and tightening it around two stakes that they set by striking with two mallets. This
scene is accompanied in Karnak by other episodes of the foundation ceremony. The King
is shown as entering the temple and introducing himself to Amūn-Rē[c], marking out a fur-
row with a hoe, moulding the foundation brick, fixing the borders of the temple together
with Seshat, and scattering natron around the temple. In the latter scene the temple is
represented as the façade of a shrine set inside an oval ring symbolizing the perimeter wall
of the sacred precinct. This scene has been copied in the temple of Amada.[69]

The meaning of some rites illustrated with temple reliefs is not yet exactly clear. Such is
the case of the ceremony called "erecting a scaffolding for a rug (cloth ?)". The rite is
depicted in scenes of Tuthmosis I on the barge-station of Amenophis I at Karnak (Pl. VI,
1-3). A sequence of three scenes comprising that of driving four calves and the King's
course, ends with the representation of a scaffolding raised between the King and the god.
This peculiar object consists of three poles of various lengths, the tallest of them standing
in the centre and being supported by two others. The ceremony takes place before the
ityphallic Amūn, but the round shrine of Min, standing behind the god, points to Amūn's
association with the god of creation and fertility. This rite[70] may be connected with a
festival of Min, but—judging by the function of the building, on which it is depicted in this
very case—it could perhaps be a part of the Opet-feast ceremonies.

Some episodes of a rite of "extinguishing torches in lakes of milk" are recorded on walls
of Theban temples.[71] A scene in the Karnak temple shows Tuthmosis III burning incense
and libating before Amūn-Rē[c], whereas a priest holding two torches stands beside two
tubs supposed to contain milk (Pl. XVI). The tubs are adorned with plants. Two huge
candelabra in the form of Nile-god figures holding torches in their hands stand before the
offering-table, between the King and the god. According to the interpretation of S. Schott,

---

[65] This interpretation has recently been proposed by F. Pawlicki who is working on a new publication on
this part of the temple.
[66] PM, II, 125, (451), 3; Barguet, Temple d'Amon-Rê, 208, note 1; LÄ, IV, 504.
[67] Aly M. and others, Amada IV, L 1-8.
[68] Barguet, Temple d'Amon-Rê, 206, pl. XXXI, A.
[69] Aly M. and others, Amada IV, L 3.
[70] LÄ, III, 454-5.
[71] Schott S., Das Löschen von Fackeln, passim.

the torch-bearers represent two guards watching the divine barge during the night.[72] The tubs of milk, supposed to be placed around the barge, would symbolise a lake on which the barge sails.[73] This rite's occurring in the sanctuary of Deir el-Bahari may point to the fact that it took place during the Feast of the Valley. This could also have been the feast, at which another ceremony was performed which was recorded in the mortuary temple of Hatshepsut (Pl. XXXIII). Tuthmosis III, wearing the ''atef''-crown, strikes a ball with a long wavy staff. The ceremony takes place before the goddess Hathor. Two priests approaching the King hold out similar balls to him. This very scene is the earliest record of this rite, and it may symbolize—particularly in later times—the King's victory over enemies. It is still possible that in the time of the XVIIIth Dynasty the scene represents but the mythicized play of the adolescent Pharaoh.[74] As the play usually takes place before Hathor, and its Deir el-Bahari version occurs in that goddess' shrine, it may be suggested that the rite was connected with a feast of Hathor or with the Feast of the Valley, which was the most important festivity on the western bank of Thebes.

Of all the religious feasts which were organized in Thebes, two of them have gained a particular renown and are frequently recorded in relief on the walls of temples. The first one is ''The Beautiful Feast of Opet'' which took place once a year in the second month of the Inundation season. It lasted for more than 10 days, and it consisted of the god's journey from Karnak to the Luxor temple and his return to the departure point. The second one is ''The Beautiful Feast of the Valley'', during which the sacred barge left the Karnak temple, crossed the Nile and visited sanctuaries on the western bank of Thebes. This feast occurred in the second month of the Harvest season (= summer), and also lasted for many days. The earliest known records of the first feast date from the XVIIIth Dynasty, whereas the second one is attested already in previous sources.[75] Our main source of information about both feasts' visual aspects before the Amarna-Period are the reliefs on the barge-shrine of Hatshepsut (the so-called ''Chapelle Rouge'') at Karnak[76] and the very fragmentarily preserved reliefs decorating the upper portico of the Deir el-Bahari temple built by the same monarch.[77]

The principal ceremony of both feasts was a procession, during which a portable barge was carried by priests on their shoulders (Pl. IX, 2; X, 3) or transported in a vessel on the Nile (Pl. IX, 1). There existed two kinds of barges. A small portable boat-shrine stood in the temple, set upon a raised base (Pl. X, 1-2; XIV, 1) or was carried by priests during processions. A river-ship of larger size carried a shrine containing the portable boat-shrine (Pl. IX, 1). Barges of both types were similar in their shape. They are skiff-like vessels with up-curving prow and stern, these being adorned with the head or a symbol of the deity to which the barge was dedicated. In Thebes that god was Amūn, and his barge stood in the Karnak temple. The barge's extremities bear his ram-head adorned with a broad collar, the ends of which have the shape of falcon-heads. Amidships on the barge stands a tall shrine for the sacred image. The portable boat-shrine, being essentially a model boat set

---

[72] LÄ, III, 1078-9.
[73] Id. Ib., 1079.
[74] LÄ, I, 608-9.
[75] LÄ, II, 181, note 173.
[76] LACAU-CHEVRIER, Chapelle, 154-204.
[77] Comp. note 36.

on a base-board upon carrying-poles, is provided with the runners of sledges (Pl. X, 1-2;
XIV, 1). Its shrine is more than half-hidden by a veil. The shrine's visible wall is
decorated with friezes of cobras and adorned with the figure of a falcon with outspread
wings. On the prow stand two goddesses: one, a "mistress of the boat" wearing a solar
disk between two horns on her head, and the goddess Maᶜet provided with a feather.[78]
Behind them there are following figures: a sphinx raised on a standard, a kneeling King
offering two bowls, and a reclining sphinx holding a vase between his front paws. Small
kneeling figures of the King support the shrine's corner-pillars, and one standing figure at
each side of the shrine represents the King as a fan-bearer. Another figure of the Pharaoh
guides the steering-oars at the stern. These wooden barges were gilded and adorned with
gems and coloured inlays.

The river-boat of Amūn, called "Userhat Amūn" ("mighty of prow is Amūn") was a
similar vessel of larger size. The walls of its shrine are decorated with friezes of alternating
pairs of "djed" and "tyet" signs (Pl. IX, 1).[79] Three tall poles are raised before the
shrine. Two of them support pictures of a falcon crowned with a solar disk with two
plumes, while the third one has the name of Hatshepsut in this place. The usual sphinx-
standard on the prow is accompanied by another one, supporting the animal of the god
Wepwaut. In the decoration of these vessels such materials were used as gold, silver, elec-
trum and cedar wood. A description of the Amūn-barge is preserved on a stela from the
mortuary temple of Amenophis III,[80] and its most detailed representation decorates the
eastern face of the 3rd pylon in Karnak, built by the same King.[81]

During the feast of Opet, Amūn of Karnak visited the sanctuary of Luxor. In the time
of Hatshepsut the journey southwards took place by land. The barge-shrine of Amūn was
carried on the shoulders of the priests and set down at intervals in wayside kiosks for
religious rituals (Pl. X, 2; XIV, 1). We are not well informed about the content and the
form of these, but the reliefs of the "Chapelle Rouge" lead us to believe that these
ceremonies comprised rites which resembled those of other feasts, e.c. incense-burning,
libating, making offerings, praying, singing, dancing, consecrating victims, the royal
route etc.[82] The feast was probably an occasion for oracular appeals or reports, and—according to the suggestion of some scholars—the god's visit to "The Southern Harîm"
could be a kind of marriage-feast, in which sexual rites played a part.[83] The journey back
to Karnak took place on the river. The portable boat-shrine containing the god's statue
was embarked upon the large "Userhat" barge and carried back to the main temple of
Amūn. The welcoming ceremonies were probably similar to those that had taken place on
the god's arrival to Luxor. The King himself participated in the feast of Opet. On the
reliefs of the "Chapelle Rouge", Hatshepsut is often accompanied by her successor
Tuthmosis III (Pl. IX, 1-3), both of them wearing analogous dresses and insignia.

"The Beautiful Feast of the Valley" started with Amūn's journey from Karnak to the
West bank of Nile. The god's portable boat-shrine crossed the river in the river-ship, after

---

[78] LACAU-CHEVRIER, Chapelle, 156.
[79] Id. Ib., 176-8.
[80] LÄ, I, 250, note 19.
[81] BARGUET, Temple d'Amon-Rê, 82, notes 1, 2; comp. HELCK in MDAIK, 37 (1981), pl. XXXVII.
[82] LACAU-CHEVRIER, Chapelle, pl. VII-IX.
[83] LÄ, IV, 576.

which it was carried by priests from one barge-station to another. One of these stations was the sanctuary of the Hatshepsut temple at Deir el-Bahari. Presided over by the King, this long festival was attended by crowds of people who followed the procession of the sacred bark and visited tombs of their relatives. In these tombs an important part of the feast's ceremonies took place. These rites are depicted in nobles' tombs, usually on the walls of their transversal halls which constitute the first room in typical XVIIIth Dynasty sepulchres. The ceremonies in the tomb were attended by the family and by friends of the deceased. They concentrated at an altar, on which various products were burning, e.c. geese or ducks, parts of animal sacrifices (heads, forelegs and ribs of beef), different sorts of bread and fruit (Pl. XXXVIII, 1-2). Upon these altars myrrh and incense were poured (Pl. XXXIX, 2). Around them were set bouquets of flowers and fruit sometimes attaining large dimensions (Pl. XLIII, 2). Their stem, composed of papyrus or lotus flowers, was adorned with poppy and, exceptionally, jasmine.[84] These bouquets were dedicated to Amūn, the protector of certain sanctuaries.[85] Besides them stood bouquets of salad (Pl. XXXVIII, 1), the holy plant and symbol of Min—the god of fertility. The altar was probably situated before the tomb, within the precincts of its court. The rites performed outside and inside the tomb comprised praying, singing, dancing and playing. Since the time of Tuthmosis IV the ceremony of burning offerings was attended by choruses of female singers coming from the temple of Amūn.[86] These participated in the procession, which entered the tomb during the Valley-feast. From the fact that these choirs were sometimes depicted on pillars inside the tomb, it may be deduced that the singers must have entered the tomb itself. Up to the time of Tuthmosis IV there were also male singers, represented with short aprons, and in later times wearing longer dresses. Male singers were often shown clapping, whereas female singers waved with their sistra and collars. Among the dances which were performed on the occasion of the festival there are even acrobatic ones. A blind harpist and singer is a frequently recorded participant of these ceremonies. Other musicians are represented with such instruments as lute, lyre, double-pipe, flute, drum and sistrum. In some early XVIIIth Dynasty tombs there are also representations of temple-guards who probably at this occasion could come over on the Western bank in order to fulfill their functions during the rituals in the tombs.[87] The ritual toilet of this feast's participants included the anointment of their bodies and putting a cone of myrrh on their heads (Pl. XLI, 1-2). The colour of these cones is red or yellow. Some participants of the feast, most frequently women, wear head-bands which may be green and red or red and white. Since the time of Amenophis II, women adorned their heads with flower-crowns, and set a single flower or just a bud upon their foreheads.[88]

Being precisely depicted in early XVIIIth Dynasty tombs, these rituals develop into a kind of general festivity of rather a secular character after the time of Tuthmosis III.[89] A revival of more religious approach towards the festival must have occurred during the time

---

[84] Schott, Das schöne Fest, 50-51.
[85] Id. Ib., 50.
[86] Id. Ib., 37.
[87] Id. Ib., 40, 47.
[88] Id. Ib., 75.
[89] Id. Ib., 85-6.

of Amenophis III, as can be deduced from the ritual character of similar scenes in his courtiers' tombs.

Among other customs connected with the festival many records mention drinking wine, probably in a kind of homage rendered to Ḥathor, the goddess of drunkenness. Deir el-Bahari, being the Theban centre of her cult, was the site of several chapels dedicated to the cow-goddess at this place (cf. Pl. XXXII, 1-2; XXXIII; XXXIV, 1). It is also probable that several statues of the deceased, which belonged to the tomb accessories, were carried in the main procession of the sacred barge during the Valley-feast.

The painted or sculptured decoration of the transverse hall in Theban nobles' tombs comprises also representations of rituals belonging to other feasts, e.c. The New Year Festival, The Harvest Festival, royal ceremonies, receptions of the tombs' owners by Kings etc. A repeatedly occurring iconographic pattern shows the serpent-headed goddess Termuthis suckling a young King (Pl. XXXV, 2) and receiving offerings from the deceased or other officials. This scene, being connected with a feast which commemorated the birth of the corn-god Neper, may constitute a mythical version of a rite which was observed during the harvest-festival.

Two parallel scenes on both sides of the entrance to the second room in many tombs represent royal ceremonies or feasts. The monarch is either receiving the tomb-owner and gratifying him with gifts or nominating him to a high office. Such events were celebrated with rites similar to those of other feasts. As the decoration of a tomb was intended to give as complete an idea as possible about the life and function of the deceased, the character of many scenes is rather general and they cannot be precisely classified as episodes of this or another feast. They may refer to those rites, in which the deceased often participated at various occasions.

The second room in an average XVIIIth Dynasty tomb has the form of a long and rather narrow corridor. On its long walls are represented scenes from funeral rituals, most frequently the transport of the deceased to a place of embalmment, to the west of Thebes and the procession of a sledge carrying the coffin. The long and complicated funeral ritual comprises 16 principal episodes, some of them being separate rituals with precisely defined acts.[90] Two of these episodes deserve particular attention and have been subjects of several studies: "The Ritual of Embalmment" and "The Ritual of Opening the Mouth". Great importance was also attached by the Egyptians to the ritual of statues (called "Pilgrimage to Abydos") and to rites of protection connected with a slaughter-ritual.

Funeral rituals in Egypt had a long tradition, dating back to the early Dynastic period. The iconographic archetypes of funeral scenes decorating the tombs of the XVIIIth Dynasty nobles also belong to the Old and Middle Kingdom. A comparative study of these pictures has been made by J. Settgast and this led to the conclusion that funeral scenes in New Kingdom tombs do not record the course of an actual ritual, but are imitations or copies of earlier tomb iconographic programme.[91] If Settgast's theory proves true, the evolution of this programme within the XVIIIth Dynasty would point more to a change in iconographic preferences than to real modifications of the ritual.[92] Three phases of this

---

[90] LÄ, I, 745-765.
[91] SETTGAST, Bestattungsdarstellungen, 112.
[92] Id. Ib., 2, 112.

evolution may be observed: a) the beginning of the XVIIIth Dynasty up to a short period following the death of Amenophis I, characterized by a continuation of Middle Kingdom patterns, which imitated Old Kingdom ritual scenes,[93] b) the time from Hatshepsut until Tuthmosis IV, the iconographic programme of its funeral scenes being a conglomeration of various scenes from earlier periods, and c) the rule of Amenophis III, bringing the first examples of a new iconographic programme, which was to be progressively developed to the end of the Dynasty and during the Ramesside Period; the former decoration patterns were now to be replaced by new artistic inventions, revealing changes that must have occurred in the ritual itself.

The whole funeral cycle lasted for about 70 days, about 52 of them being reserved for cleaning the corpse, followed by its mummification. The repertory of funeral scenes in every tomb constitutes a choice of the ritual's various episodes. The composition, sequence and iconographic details of these scenes however follow some fixed patterns. Some groups of scenes, repeatedly occurring in tombs of similar date, may be distinguished. Particular versions of the funeral cycle are recorded in Theban tombs N[os] 20 (Mentuḥirkhopshef) and 29 (Amenemōpet).[94]

The ritual started with carrying the corpse in a coffin from the house of the deceased to the boat, in which it was transported to the embalmment-hall. The ceremony of leaving the house could be accompanied by the burning of incense. The embalmment took place in a building called "divine kiosk of Anubis", situated on the western bank of the river. The ritual of embalmment comprised both religious and practical acts. After being cleaned with natron and wrapped in embalmed bandages, the corpse was placed in a coffin and thus carried to a boat. Then followed a "journey to Sais", i.e. to a sacred place within the Valley. In this ceremony various priests participated, reciting religious spells. There occurred an interval on the way at an altar, where offering-rites were performed. In New Kingdom records this place is called "The Hall of Unification". The next sacred place to be visited by the coffin's procession was a necropolis called "Buto". This episode belongs to the most frequently represented ones. The coffing is shown as being dragged on sledges by oxen and, additionally, by men holding a rope attached to the sledge. In some cases water, incense or milk are offered to the deceased on the way.[95] Accompanied by mourners of both sexes and by dignitaries, the coffin-procession arrived at the necropolis, where it is welcomed by the "muu" dancers. These were always men, often wearing a characteristic headdress which is a kind of tall crown made of reeds and resembling the hub of the "atef"-crown.[96] A particularity of this rite's XVIIIth Dynasty versions is that instead of the crown-wearing "muu", there often occurred a pair of dancers without crowns. The dancers set the coffin on a shrine-boat, after which follows a procession to places associated with Heliopolis. The next rites occurred in the tomb's precincts. The mummy, removed from the boat, was placed before the tomb or put on a stretcher. Mourning women approach the mummy, whereas a priest performed its purification with a "nemset"-jug. This rite is followed by the "Ritual of Opening the Mouth", and by the

---

[93] Id. Ib., 2, 112.
[94] Davies, Five Theban Tombs, pl. II, VI-X and XLIII; comp. LÄ, I, 748.
[95] LÄ, I, 755-6.
[96] Brunner-Traut, Der Tanz, 53; comp. LÄ, IV, 271-2.

burning of incense. The ritual was addressed either to a statue or to the mummy, and
sometimes possibly to the inner coffin of the deceased.

In its complete version, the ''Ritual of Opening the Mouth'' was composed of 75
episodes comprising such acts as pouring water on the mummy or the statue, burning incense to various gods and the mummy, slaughtering an animal and offering its foreleg and
heart, opening the mouth with different instruments, dressing and adorning the statue (or
the mummy), anointing, introducing a ''son who loves'' (or a priest playing his role), liba-
tions, touching the mummy with a finger etc., ending with the transportation of the mummy into the tomb or that of the statue into a chapel. The final scene shows the ''sem''
priest performing the ''nini''-purification.[97] A great variety of objects was used during
these ceremonies. These objects are depicted on a fragmentary stela remaining until now
in the court of the Theban tomb N° 57 (Khaᶜ emḥēt, temp. Amenophis III: Pl. XXXVI,
2). Besides the usual ritual equipment there are several objects connected particularly with
the ''Ritual of Opening the Mouth'', among which various sorts of hatchets and scissors,
a ''golden finger'', a serpent-shaped baton with a ram's head (called ''wert-heka'' =
''great of magic'') and a knife with a split blade resembling the tail of fish (called ''pesesh-
kaf'').[98]

These ceremonies were performed by various sorts of priests and artisans. Practical
functions were in charge of the ''sem''-priest (Pl. XL), whereas a lecturer-priest (''kheri-
heb'') recited religious spells from a papyrus-roll. Among other priests there was a ''son
who loves'', identified with Osiris' son Horus, and ''nine friends'' carrying the statue or
the coffin.[99] Although the ceremonies took place in or before the tomb, the texts recall
other sacred places, in which this ritual could occur in earlier times or on the occasion of
''opening the mouth'' performed on other objects than the mummy. The ritual's aim was
to vivify the object, therefore not only statues and mummies, but also shawabti-figures,
scarabs, sacred animals, barks and temples were subject to these rites.[100] The ritual was
also mythicized and transferred to the other world as part of the ''Book of the Dead''.

Theban tombs of the XVIIIth Dynasty provide different kinds of records connected with
rites of ''opening the mouth'': a) sequences of scenes referring to the ritual itself, the most
complete version being preserved in the tomb of Rekhmirēᶜ (Theban tomb N° 100); b)
one single scene representing an episode with the statue of the deceased or with his coffin— a kind of ''label'' for the whole ritual (cf. Pl. XXXVI, 1); c) representations of rites
resembling some episodes of the opening-ritual, but performed on the person of the
deceased, sometimes accompanied by his wife (cf. Pl. XXXVII; XL, 1-2), popular since
the time of Amenophis II[101]; d) abbreviated versions of scenes representing only one officiant and the coffin or the statue which in some cases is replaced by the deceased
himself.[102]

Next scenes of the funeral cycle depicted in Egyptian tombs refer to rites with the coffin
and with the statue. The coffin is first dragged on a sledge by priests. According to the ac-

---

[97] Otto, Mundöffnungsritual, Szene 75.
[98] Cf. Bibliography by Walsem R. van.
[99] Goyon, Rituels funéraires, 96-9.
[100] Id. Ib., 90, note 1; comp. LÄ, IV, 224.
[101] Otto, Mundöffnungsritual, 30.
[102] Id. Ib., 30.

companying text, one of them drags it to the North, and the other one—to the South. Following episodes are the procession of a ritual object called ''tekenu'' and a rite of incense burning. The ''tekenu'' was a figure dragged on sledge, and representing the bull of the sun-god. This role was played by a priest wrapped in a leather-cloak, and either pear-shaped, h.e. reclining folded forwards, or squatting upright on the sledge. It has been suggested that this priest retained a prominent position in the cattle-benches of the ''Sais''-place in the necropolis.[103] A foe of the sun-bull appears in the next scene as a divinity, which may be associated with the approaching slaughtering-ceremony. This divinity sometimes occurs in a scene of incense burning, and is sometimes subject to the rite of painting its eyes.[104] The procession of ''tekenu'' is usually accompanied by that of ''canopic jars'' containing the entrails of the deceased. The jars are set in a box dragged on a sledge by many people. A lecturer-priest presides over the procession and recites appropriate spells. Both the ''tekenu''-procession and that of canopic jars start in the ''Sais'' of the necropolis, and take place simultaneously with or slightly later than the cortège of the coffin. All these processions approach the tomb, h.e. the ''Buto''-place, where they are welcomed by the crown-wearing ''muu'' or by a pair of other dancers. Their participants then attend a ritual of offerings, performed at a place marked by a false door stela. Offering-ritual consisted of bringing the various products enumerated in the list of offerings. These products are sometimes carried on offering-mats or in boxes set on carrying-poles, and sometimes dragged on a sledge. After this ceremony follows the episode of bringing funeral equipment, comprising statues, furniture, clothing, jewellery, amulets, insignia, weapons, ointments, flowers etc. (cf. Pl. XXIV, 2).[105] At the end of all offering-rituals occurs the sacrificial slaughtering of an animal somewhere in the necropolis, and the bringing of its heart and foreleg to the tomb (Pl. XXXV, 1) in order to burn it on an altar. Scenes closing the funeral cycle show the transportation of the coffin from the offering-place to the tomb by the ''nine friends'' encountered in the ritual of opening the mouth. This moment is again connected with censing and libating.

A particular part of funeral ceremonies consists in a procession of the statues, and is called ''the pilgrimage to Abydos'' (Pl. XLII and XLIII, 1). Two statues representing the deceased and his wife are placed in a shrine standing in the middle of a barge, which is towed by another vessel. An offering-table is set in front of the shrine, at which a priest performs ritual acts. The barge is usually depicted twice, once at the journey to, and once at the return from ''Abydos''. It seems that the title of the ritual is merely metaphoric, ''Abydos'' being probably a sacred place within the necropolis, in the same way as ''Sais'' or ''Buto''. The rite might have been just a journey of the statues within the necropolis, symbolizing or recalling the deceased's real pilgrimage to Abydos.[106] There are iconographic differences between scenes of the pilgrimage in early XVIIIth Dynasty tombs up to the reign of Hatshepsut, and those of her successors' time. In the early examples the statue of the deceased alternates with his mummy,[107] whereas in later records always occur the two statues (Pl. XLII and XLIII, 1).

---

[103] LÄ, I, 758.
[104] LÄ, I, 759.
[105] LÄ, I, 760-1.
[106] LÄ, I, 47.
[107] LÄ, I, 44.

Final ceremonies of the funeral cycle took place in a "house of pillars", which is once described as "the first gate of the other world".[108] Priests recited there various spells granting protection to the deceased. This house was situated within the necropolis. Another ritual connected with the protection of the dead occurred simultaneously in the "holy district" of the necropolis. This was the slaughtering-ritual, in which the "tekenu"-figure retained an important role.

The described version of funeral ceremonies is attested in the nobles' tombs. Egyptians belonging to lower social classes were supposedly buried according to a simplified ritual, perhaps just a kind of "pilgrimage to Abydos".

The accessible parts of each tomb were destined for the cult of the deceased. That was the place where the present life made contact with the other world. A chapel situated in each tomb's western extremity, at the end of a corridor, contained a statue of the deceased, in front of which offerings were deposited. This chapel was the principal cult place in funeral rites. Secondary cult-places were situated at both extremities of the transversal hall in the tomb's frontal part. On the two short walls closing this hall at its south and north sides there were stelae, false-door stelae and niches for statues. Usually one of these walls (most frequently the southern one) housed the false-door, whereas a stela was situated on the parallel wall. In some tombs a second stela replaced the false-door.[109] False doors were symbolic entrances to the other world, through which the deceased made contact with the world of the living ones. The stela commemorated important facts concerning the deceased and was a kind of manifest illustrated by the double-scene in its upper part. The scene usually shows the deceased, either praying and making an offering before the gods or an offering to the King, or else sitting at an offering-table and receiving offerings from members of his family. The symmetrical construction of these scenes was an occasion to demonstrate the antithetic parallelism of some gods, such as Osiris and Anubis, Isis and Nephthys, the Eastern and Western goddesses, Ḥathor and other goddesses (cf. Maˁet), Rēˁ-Ḥarakhti and Atum etc. Similar scenes occur on lintels above the doors connecting subsequent parts of the tombs. It belongs to the inventions of the XVIIIth Dynasty religious iconography that non-royal subjects could be depicted together with gods of the other world.[110] The upper part of funeral stelae was decorated with emblems belonging to the vast repertory of religious symbols.[111] Since the time of Amenophis III the stelae on the short walls of the transversal rooms are sometimes replaced by niches for statues. The earliest known example of this concept occurs in the tomb of Khaˁemḥēt (Thebes, N° 57). Another innovation dating back to the time of this King concerns the place, in which was depicted the "ritual of opening the mouth". Scenes of this ritual have then been transferred from the tomb's interior to its court (cf. Pl. XXXVI, 2). These changes point to a possible modification of the funeral ritual during the reign of Amenophis III. The opening-ritual could since that time have occurred outside the tomb, and the short walls, reserved previously for stelae, could have been transformed into an additional cult-place with a statue set inside a niche.[112]

---

[108] LÄ, I, 762.
[109] HERMANN, Stelen, 27.
[110] Id. Ib., 53.
[111] Id. Ib., 53-63.
[112] Id. Ib., 99-100.

Two types of statues are attested as cult-pictures in the XVIIIth Dynasty nobles' tombs: a) representations of the deceased seated with one or two members of his family, and b) a figure of the deceased kneeling and holding a stela.[113] Statues of the nobles adorned also Egyptian temples. Among common types of the XVIIIth Dynasty statuary there are cubiform figures of squatting individuals[114] and statues that show a kneeling official holding a ritual object, e.g. an offering-basin[115] or a bundle of rope adorned with a crowned ram-head of Amūn.[116] A group of particular iconographic features constitute numerous statues of Sen-en-mut, the chief steward of Hatshepsut.[117]

Statues of gods and Kings belonged both to the funeral equipment and to the temple decoration. They were made of different materials including stone, wood, metals and faience. Their dimensions vary according to their functions. Colossal stone statues adorned the entrance to Egyptian temples. Gods were depicted either in their animal form (cf. crocodile, Pl. XLVII, 1, a-b)[118] or as composite figures combining a human body with an animal's head (cf. Pl. XLVII, 2, a-b). To the latter category belongs a large group of statues representing the lioness-headed Sekhmet, produced in the time of Amenophis III for the Karnak-temple of Mut.[119]

Royal statues show the King either as a human being or as human-headed sphinx. In the first case the monarch is represented in one of his typical attitudes known from ritual scenes: throning,[120] standing[121] or kneeling and offering a ritual object. Among the objects held by the King two small globular jars occur the most frequently.[122] In sporadic cases the King holds an offering-plate,[123] one jar combined with a "djed"-pillar[124] of fish.[125] The King is usually wearing a "nemes"- or "khat"-headdress; other crowns and wigs occur less frequently. It is not until the time of Amenophis III that a monarch was represented in statuary as wearing the "blue crown" ("khepresh").[126] This King's statues reveal some more iconographic innovations, including the prototype of statues showing a prostrating Pharaoh.[127] A short apron and a collar constitute the King's usual dress. In few cases the monarch wears the so-called falcon-dress[128] or a long ceremonial coat associated with the "sed" feast.[129]

The most popular type of royal statuary depicts the King alone. Less frequently he is shown accompanied by members of his family, e.c. mother[130] or wife and children.[131] A

---

[113] HAYES, Scepter, II, 160, fig. 88.
[114] GÖTTER. PHARAONEN, Nr. 29.
[115] MÜLLER, Ägyptische Kunst, 102.
[116] GÖTTER. PHARAONEN, Nr. 30.
[117] Cf. Bibliography by BOTHMER B.V.; comp. HAYES, Scepter, II, 106, fig. 57; MÜLLER, Ägyptische Kunst, 99.
[118] E.c. lion; MÜLLER, op. cit., 116.
[119] PM, II, 262-8; comp. HAYES, Scepter, II, 238, fig. 143.
[120] E.c. HAYES, Scepter, II, 98, fig. 54 and 234-5, fig. 139-140; MÜLLER, Ägyptische Kunst, 118.
[121] E.c. HAYES, Scepter, II, 95, fig. 52 and 120, fig. 62.
[122] E.c. HAYES, op. cit., 96, fig. 53 and 143, fig. 79; MÜLLER, op. cit., 107.
[123] LÄ, III, 570, note 260.
[124] LÄ, III, 569, fig. 2.
[125] LÄ, III, 570, note 238 and 571, note 279.
[126] LÄ, III, 571, notes 280-1.
[127] LÄ, III, 571, note 289.
[128] LÄ, III, 570, note 242 and 571, notes 274, 288.
[129] LÄ, III, 570, notes 240, 258 and 571, note 283.
[130] LÄ, III, 571, note 272.
[131] LÄ, III, 571, note 290.

triad of Tuthmosis I shows the King together with his famous grandmother Aḥmose-Nefertere and Amūn.[132] A unique statue of Hatshepsut represents the Queen on her nurse's lap.[133] The iconography of royal sphinges reveals some particularities in the time of Hatshepsut and Amenophis III. An invention of the Queen's artists was the type of sphinx with mane,[134] whereas those of Amenophis introduced the kind of sphinx holding a ritual object with his frontal paws,[135] and a winged sphinx.[136]

Many statues show the King in the company of one or two gods. Two types may be distinguished in this group: diads (Pl. XLVII, 2, a-b) or triads of the usual type,[137] and statues showing a King protected by a divine animal, cf. a falcon,[138] the Ḥathor-cow,[139] the Maᶜet-snake,[140] the Amūn-ram[141] or the Anubis-jackal[142].

A singular group constitute the so-called Osiride statues of Kings. They decorated frontal faces of pillars in temple porticoes or stood in niches and in the sanctuary, cf. at Deir el-Bahari.[143] They represent the King in the guise of the mummified Osiris holding his usual insignia in his hands crossed on the breast.

Another important set of statues belonged to the funeral equipment of royal tombs. Several objects of this kind have been found in the Valley of the Kings, and their representations decorate the tombs' walls.[144] There were usually figures of various gods (cf. Isis, Nephthys, Sekhmet, the Sons of Horus, Tatenen, Atum, Geb etc.), standards with pictures of falcon-, snake-, and crocodile-gods, statues representing the King standing (sometimes on a panther or in a papyrus-boat), a youth holding sistra, a goose (usually made of black wood), a cow's head or a "Ka"-standard. According to their religious symbolism and function, these statues have been attributed by F. Abitz to four different groups: a) ritual objects, b) objects symbolising the revival, c) personification of rejuvenation, and d) symbols of ascension to the sky.[145]

Other objects of typically funeral function and belonging to the tombs' equipment were the coffin, the canopic (or visceral) jars and the shawabti-figures. The coffins of the period from the XVIIIth Dynasty on were anthropoid in shape. Up to the reign of Tuthmosis III their painted decoration represents the wings of a vulture spread protectively over the body. A broad collar is represented on the chest. Down the middle of the lid, between the wings of the vulture, a band is left for the inscription.[146] The feathered decoration of anthropoid coffins disappeared by the time of Tuthmosis III, being replaced by black coffin with yellow or gold bands of inscription. Royal sarcophagi of the XVIIIth Dynasty were

---

[132] LÄ, III, 568, note 212.
[133] LÄ, III, 569, note 226.
[134] LÄ, III, 569, note 228.
[135] LÄ, III, 571, note 301.
[136] LÄ, III, 571, note 302.
[137] LÄ, III, 570, notes 245-7, 249-250 and 571, notes 291-2.
[138] LÄ, III, 570, note 241.
[139] LÄ, III, 570, note 262.
[140] GÖTTER, PHARAONEN, Nr. 27.
[141] LÄ, III, 570, note 264 and 571, note 297.
[142] LÄ, III, 571, note 298.
[143] PM, II, 372-3; comp. MÜLLER, Ägyptische Kunst, 92-3; HAYES, Scepter, II, 90, 92, 93, fig. 49-51.
[144] ABITZ, Statuetten, 55 ff.
[145] Id. Ib., 121.
[146] HAYES, Scepter, II, 30, 221.

rectangular stone boxes decorated with reliefs representing gods and with texts from the "Book of the Dead.[147] The canopic jars of Thutmoside date are provided with stoppers in the form of a human head. Their faces were painted red or yellow, according to the sex of the owner.[148] These jars were deposited in sets of four in the interiors of shrine-shaped canopic chests which were mounted on sledge runners.[149] Shawabti figures of the period retain the characteristics of their Middle Kingdom predecessors, being mummified representations of their deceased owners. Their hands appear crossed over their chests, and they often hold hoes, baskets or other implements (copper axe, copper mattock, model yoke, pair of flat bags) which were either carved in relief on the surface of the figures or made separately—usually of metal—and inserted into holes of the figure's clenched fists.[150]

Functioning as compendia of Egyptian ideas about the other world, were some "books" invented at the beginning of the XVIIIth Dynasty. Two of them became popular before the Amarna Period: "The Book of the Dead" (known to Egyptians as the "Chapters of Coming-forth by Day") and the "Amduat" (i.e. "The Book of What is in the Underworld"). Both of them are composed of texts and illustrations. Although the "Book of the Dead" has its literary archetype in the "Coffin Texts" of the Middle Kingdom, it was only from the beginning of the New Kingdom that these religious spells were accompanied by "vignettes", some of which became real masterpieces of Egyptian painting. Various chapters of the "Book" were usually written on papyri and deposited in burial chambers together with the mummy. The earliest known versions of the "Book" are preserved on the few papyri dating back to the mid XVIIIth Dynasty: Iouya, Kha[c] and Nu.[151] They were found in the tombs of their owners. Some of the most popular vignettes could be reproduced in larger size on the tomb's walls. These items include e.g. the funeral procession and the ceremonies at the tomb (illustrations to Chapter 1), agricultural scenes occurring in the so-called "Fields of Iaru" (Chapter 110), the chapter of the so-called sepulchral chamber (151 A—e.g. Pl. XXV, 1), the judgement of the deceased in the Hall of Osiris (Chapter 125), the bull with seven cows and Anubis with divine oars (Chapter 148), the adoration of Osiris by the deceased (Chapter 185—e.g. Pl. XXXI, 1-2) and others. The illustrations to the "Book" comprise both mythicized rituals and representations of mythological scenes.

The "Amduat" constitutes a version of the underworld that before the Amarna Period was reserved for the King. This book was usually painted on the walls of burial chambers in royal tombs. Its earliest known copy persists in some fragments from the tomb of Tuthmosis I.[152] An abbreviated version of the book could exceptionally have decorated the tombs of the highest non-royal personages in the Egyptian hierarchy.[153] The form of the "Amduat" has possibly been inspired by that of the "Book of the Two Ways". "Amduat" is composed of 12 divisions, which were a transposition of the 12 hours of the

---

[147] HAYES, Royal Sarcophagi, passim.
[148] HAYES, Scepter, II, 228, fig. 135.
[149] Id. Ib., 227, fig. 134.
[150] Id. Ib., 229.
[151] BARGUET, Le Livre des Morts, 11.
[152] HORNUNG, Amduat, I, Text, XIII.
[153] Cf. Bibliography by HORNUNG, Die Grabkammer.

night. Each division comprises 3 registers, the middle one being reserved for the sacred barge of the sun-god, who is represented as a human being with ram's head (Pl. XXIX, 1-2). He is described as "Flesh of Rēꜥ". This scheme of composition is broken but within two divisions: the 4th (Pl. XXVIII, 2) and the 5th (Pl. XXV, 2), where diagonal paths cross the fields of horizontal registers. The book depicts the wandering of the sun-god through the nether world during the night. The journey starts with the god's entry into the other world in the evening. Many other gods are represented as jubilating at this moment.[154] Osiris occurs in the "book" as a nightly form of the sun-god (Pl. XXVI, 1; XXIX, 1—upper register), and Sokari is represented in his domain of "Ro-setau" (Pl. XXV, 2). From the seventh division onwards the sun-god's barge is accompanied by a protective snake called Meḥen. The last episode of the "book" shows the god's rebirth in the morning. In this act, he is also accompanied by his friends. The eschatological meaning of the "Amduat" may, therefore, be presumed as the wish of the dead to accompany Rēꜥ during the night in order to revive with him every day. In this aspect "Amduat" repeats the main idea of the "Book of the Dead": an identification of the deceased with the sun, and his hope to gain the capacity of "coming-forth by day".

The sketchy form of the figures in early versions of "Amduat", up to the reign of Amenophis III, became an argument in favour of the hypothesis that the decoration of royal tombs of this period was literally copied from papyri. The "list of gods" occurring in the "Amduat" is painted in the tomb of Tuthmosis III on the walls of the room preceding its burial chamber (Pl. XXVI; XXVII, XXVIII, 1). This illustrated "dictionary", unique in its kind, may be interpreted as an Ancient Egyptian study of religious iconography related to the other world of the King.

Religious items constitute an important element of the hieroglyphic writing (cf. Pl. XLVIII, 2-3), and they often occur as decorative motifs on various objects (e.c. vases, pectorals, furniture etc., cf. Pl. XLVIII, 1). As such they would deserve a particular study which is not the aim of this introdution.

Constituting a vast complex of similar religious monuments, the Theban necropolis provides a continuous documentary sequence for the study of religious iconography in its evolution during the New Kingdom era. This material is the best illustration of iconographic changes that permit us to divide the period preceding the reign of Amenophis IV into three phases:

a) from the beginning of the XVIIIth Dynasty up to the time of Hatshepsut: the continuation of Middle Kingdom traditions;

b) between Hatshepsut and Tuthmosis IV: secularisation of the ritual and eclectic trends in religious iconography;

c) the reign of Amenophis III: a revival of religious interests and the appearance of new iconographic tendencies.

---

[154] Hornung, Amduat, I, Erste Stunde.

CATALOGUE OF ILLUSTRATIONS

Plate I

The King receiving the symbols of life and stability from the god Amūn-Rēᶜ:
1. King Amosis with wife and son before the god. Limestone stela found in Karnak. Now in Karnak store. (PM, II, 73; ASAE, 56, 1959, 139 sq., pls. I, II).
2. King Amenophis III with the god. Fragment of a sandstone block from a Theban temple. Now in the ḥeb-sed temple of Amenophis II in Karnak. Dimensions: H.-74 cm, w.-95 cm. (PM, II, 186, finds).

Plate II

The King as a heir of the falcon-god Horus:
1. The falcon Beḥdety—a form of Horus. Fragmentary relief on a limestone block from the ḥeb-sed temple of Amenophis I in Karnak. Upper part of a pillar. Height of the block: 44 cm. Open-air museum in Karnak. (PM, II, 134).
2. Amenophis III protected by the falcon-god. A relief in the tomb of Kheruef, Thebes West (Nr. 192). Limestone. (PM, I,₁, sec. ed., 299 /8/; The Epigraphic Survey, Chicago, pl. 48-9, text p. 54-6).

Plate III

The vulture-goddess Nekhbet associated with Queen-mother:
1. Nekhbet-bird as the crowning of a ritual scene. Relief on another face of the block (Pl. II, 1) in Karnak. (PM, II, 134).
2. Queen Tetisheri, grandmother of King Amosis, wearing the vulture headdress. Upper part of a limestone stela found in Abydos. Egyptian Museum, Cairo, CG 34002. (PM, V, 92).
3. Queen Aḥmose, mother of Queen Hatshepsut. Relief in the temple of Hatshepsut, Deir el-Bahari. Limestone (PM, II, 365/129/).

Plate IV

King Amenophis I offering to ityphallic Amūn-Rēᶜ:
1) bread, 2) scepter "sekhem", 3) lettuce, 4) "nu"-bowls.   Reliefs from the ḥeb-sed temple of Amenophis I in Karnak. Limestone. Open-air museum in Karnak.
1)-3)- three faces of a block from the lower part of a pillar. Dimensions of the block: h.-79 cm, w.- 64 cm. Height of the King: 56 cm.
4) block from the lower part of a similar pillar. (PM, II, 134).

Plate V

Royal ceremonies:
1. Ḥeb-sed scene on the outer lintel from a temple of Amenophis I in Karnak. Sandstone. Open-air museum in Karnak. (PM, II, 133-4).

2. The coronation of Tuthmosis III. Relief on the pyramidion of the granite obelisk A, lying in court of the Amūn-temple, Karnak. (PM, II, 74, court between third and fourth pylons).

Plate VI

King Tuthmosis I in ritual scenes with god Amūn:
1. Driving four calves to Amūn-Kamutf.
2. Running with oar and "ḥap"-object (part of steering gear of ships).
3. Erecting the pole of a tent.
Reliefs on the bark-shrine of Amenophis I in Karnak. Exterior, south side. Alabaster. Karnak, open-air museum. (PM, II, 63).

Plate VII

The King offering four victims to Amūn:
1. Hatshepsut in a scene from the "Chapelle Rouge", Karnak. Quartzite. Block Nr. 150. Open-air museum, Karnak. (Lacau-Chevrier, Chapelle, p. 276-8, §§ 444-446, pl. 14, assise 3).
2. Relief of Tuthmosis III on his alabaster bark-shrine in Karnak. (PM, II, 173/514/, 1).

Plate VIII

Queen Hatshepsut with gods in ritual scenes. "Chapelle Rouge", Karnak. Open-air museum.
1. Running with "ḥes"-vases to Amūn-Rēᶜ. Block Nr. 150 (Lacau-Chevrier, Chapelle, p. 274, § 439, pl. 14, assise 3).
2. With goddess Seshat in the rite of founding a temple. Block Nr. 311 (Id.Ib. p. 269, § 424, pl. 13. assise 2).

Plate IX

Sacred barks at festivities. "Chapelle Rouge", Karnak. Open-air museum.
1. Tuthmosis III rowing "Userhat", the river-bark of Amūn. Block Nr. 104. (Lacau-Chevrier, Chapelle, p. 175-191, §§ 241-275, pl. 9, assise 5).
2. The portable bark-shrine leaving a bark-station. Block Nr. 169. (Id. Ib., p. 166-7, §§ 219-221, pl. 7, assise 3).
3. Hatshepsut and Tuthmosis III attending a procession of the divine bark. Block Nr. 26. (Id. Ib., p. 161-4, §§ 207-215, pl. 7, assise 3).

Plate X

Rites performed in front of the bark of Amūn: "Chapelle Rouge", Karnak. Open-air museum.
1. Hatshepsut offering two "nu"-jugs in front of an offering-table. Block Nr. 260. (Lacau-Chevrier, Chapelle, p. 355-6, §§ 620-623, pl. 20, assise 5).
2. Hatshepsut running with the bull Apis to a bark-station. Block Nr. 102. (Id. Ib., p. 194-8, §§ 285-294, pl. 9, assise 5).
3. Hatshepsut consecrating four "meret"-boxes to the bark leaving a festival-hall. Block Nr. 303. (Id. Ib., p. 191-4, §§ 276-282, pl. 9, assise 5).

Plate XI

Tuthmosis III offering to Amūn. Reliefs on walls of the Karnak temple. Sandstone.
1. Consecrating four "meret"-boxes of coloured cloth (?). Festival-temple of Tuthmosis III. (PM, II, 117/377/, II, 4).
2. Dedicating treasure to Amūn. Room XVIII south of granite sanctuary. (PM, II, 105/319/).

Plate XII

Scenes of daily ritual in the temple of Karnak. Karnak, temple of Amūn, room XXIII south of granite sanctuary. Sandstone.
1. Tuthmosis II purifying Amūn with four "nmst"-jugs. (PM, II, 106/ 326/, (a), 1-2).
2. Tuthmosis II touching the god. (Id. Ib., 106/326/, (a), 4).

Plate XIII

Tuthmosis III purifying a statue of Amūn-Rēꜥ. Karnak, festival temple of Tuthmosis III. Sandstone.
1. Purification with four "dšrt"-jugs. Room XXI of Sokari.(PM, II, 117/378/, I, 3-4).
2. Presenting incense to and pouring water on the statue. Corridor XL. (Id. Ib., 123/432/, western part).

Plate XIV

Tuthmosis III censing. Reliefs on walls of Karnak temples.
1. Before the bark of Amūn standing in the fifth bark-station. "Chapelle Rouge". Quartzite. Block Nr. 169. Karnak, open-air museum.(Lacau-Chevrier, Chapelle, p. 166-7, §§ 219-221, pl. 7, assise 3).
2. In front of god Ptah standing in his shrine. Temple of Ptah. Sandstone. (PM, II, 199,/15/).

Plate XV

Tuthmosis III in ritual scenes with Ptah. Karnak, temple of Ptah. Sandstone.
1. Offering natron to the god. (PM, II, 201,/28/, (b), 1).
2. The King embraced by the god. (Id. Ib., 201,/28/, (c), 2).

Plate XVI

The rite of extinguishing torches in lakes of milk. Karnak. Relief of Tuthmosis III in his festival temple. Corridor XL. Sandstone. (PM, II, 123, /432/, eastern part/.

Plate XVII

Amūn-Rēꜥ granting life to the King. Reliefs on walls of Karnak temples.
1. Tuthmosis III led by god Monthu to Amūn giving life. Enclosure of Tuthmosis III, court between fifth and sixth pylons. Granite. (PM, II, 86,/224/, II).
2. Amenophis II embraced by the god. Ḥeb-sed temple of the King. Eastern row of pillars, southern pillar. (PM, II, 186, pillars).

Plate XVIII

Emblems symbolizing the unification of Lower and Upper Egypt. Reliefs decorating walls of Karnak temples. Sandstone.
1. Block with names of Tuthmosis I, from above a door. Found and exposed in the temple of Amūn. Dimensions of the block: h.- 1,30 m; w.- 1,65 m. Height of the scene: 0,85 m. (Barguet, Temple d'Amon-Rê, pl. XII, A).
2. Religious motifs on the base of a royal shrine with throne of Sesostris I. Temp. Tuthmosis III. South passage of rooms constructed by Hatshepsut, south of granite sanctuary. (PM, II, 107,/330/).

Plate XIX

King smiting foreign people before Amūn. Reliefs decorating pylons of the Amūn temple in Karnak. Sandstone.
1. Tuthmosis III smiting Asiatic captives before Amūn, with 119 name-rings. VIIth pylon, south face.(PM II, 170/499/).
2. Amenophis II smiting captives. VIIIth pylon, south face. (PM, II, 176/522/).

Plate XX

The Egyptian King and his foreign enemies.
1. Tuthmosis IV slaying captives. Detail of the scene. Relief in leather on stucco, decorating the chariot found in the King's tomb (Valley of the Kings, N° 43). Now in Egyptian Museum, Cairo, JE 46097. (PM, I,₂, sec. ed., 560, finds/chariot/).
2. Foreigners in symbolical scenes decorating the throne of Amenophis III and the base of his kiosk. Relief in the tomb of Khaᶜemḥēt (Thebes West, N° 57). Limestone. (PM, I,₁ sec. ed., 115/11/).

Plate XXI

The royal sphinx and foreign captives.
1. Tuthmosis IV represented as sphinx, trampling foes. Detail of the scene. Relief on the King's chariot (same as Pl. XX, 1).
2. Asiatic, Libyan and Nubian people with their ring-names. Relief in the tomb of Kheruef (Thebes West, N° 192). Limestone. (PM, I, sec. ed., 299/8/; The Epigraphic Survey, Chicago, pl. 48-9, 58 A, text p. 55).

Plate XXII

Procession of royal family and royal statues.
1. Royal family approaching the tree-goddess suckling Tuthmosis III. Drawing (black and red ink) on a pillar in the tomb of Tuthmosis III (Valley of the Kings, N° 34). Limestone. (PM, I,₂ sec. ed., 553, pillar A,/ b/).
2. Statues of the royal family including Tuthmosis III and his wife, Queen Sitiᶜoḥ. Relief on a sandstone block from the festival temple of Tuthmosis III in Karnak. Now exhibited in corridor XL, A of the temple. (PM, II, 124,/436/).

Plate XXIII

The deification of the King. Reliefs on votive stelae.
1. Sesostris I and Tuthmosis III represented as parallel gods seated at an offering table. Limestone stela. Origin unknown. Fitzwilliam Museum, Cambridge, EGA. 3074. 1943. Dimensions: h.- 22 cm, w.- 16 cm. Unpublished.
2. Deified Tuthmosis II receiving offerings. Limestone stela from Deir el-Medina. Museo Egizio di Torino, N° 1458.(M. Tosi, A. Roccati, Stele e altre epigrafi di Deir el-Medina, Torino, 1972, n° 50003, p. 34).

Plate XXIV

Processions of offering-bringers.
1. Singers and priests with ritual objects in the Karnak temple. Relief in the festival temple of Tuthmosis III, corridor XL. Sandstone. (PM, II, 123/432/, 3).
2. Procession of men bringing funeral equipment. Polychrome painting in the tomb of Sennūfer (Thebes West, N° 96). Temp. Amenophis II. (PM, I,$_1$, sec. ed., 200,/ 27/-/ 28/, I).

Plate XXV

Great religious books in the world of the dead. Paintings on walls of Theban tombs.
1. Fragment of the "Book of the Dead" (Chapter 151 A). Tomb of Sennūfer (Thebes West, N° 96). Temp. Amenophis II. (PM, I,$_1$, sec. ed., 202,/37/).
2. Fragment of the "Amduat" book. Fifth division including the lake of fire. Tomb of Tuthmosis III (Valley of the Kings, N° 34). (PM, I,$_2$, sec. ed., 553, sarcophagus chamber H).

Plate XXVI

Some divinities of the "Amduat". Drawings in the tomb of Tuthmosis III (Valley of the Kings, N° 34). From the "list of divinities" on walls of the room F.
1. Flesh of Osiris.
2. Flesh of Atum.
3. Thoth.
4. God of many faces. (PM, I,$_2$, sec. ed., 553, room F).

Plate XXVII

Two-headed gods of the "Amduat". Fragments of the "list of divinities" in the tomb of Tuthmosis III (Valley of the Kings, N° 34). Drawings on the walls of room F. (PM, I,$_2$ sec. ed., 553, room F).

Plate XXVIII

The world of the "Amduat". Drawings on walls in the tomb of Tuthmosis III (Valley of the Kings, N° 34).
1. Dwellers of the other world in different attitudes. From the "list of divinities" represented on the walls of room F. (PM, I,$_2$, sec. ed., 553, room F).

2. Sand-ways and water-basins in the fourth division of "Amduat". Sarcophagus chamber H. (PM, I,₂, sec. ed., 553, chamber H).

Plate XXIX

The solar god wandering in the other world. "Amduat" book painted on walls of the sarcophagus chamber in the tomb of Tuthmosis III (Valley of the Kings, N° 34).
1. Seventh division of "Amduat".
2. Eleventh division of "Amduat". (PM, I,₂, sec. ed., 553, chamber H).

Plate XXX

Solar god and Osiris—two opposite aspects of the other world.
1. Forms of the solar deity as represented in the tomb of Tuthmosis III (Valley of the Kings, N° 34). Drawing on pillar A in sarcophagus chamber. (PM, I,₂ sec. ed., 553, pillar A/ d/).
2. Osiris and the Western goddess. Relief in the tomb of Kha^cemḥēt (Thebes West, N° 57). Limestone. (PM, I,₁, sec. ed., 117/19/).

Plate XXXI

Adoration of Osiris in the West.
1. Osiris and Anubis adored by tomb owner and his wife. Painting on wall of the tomb of Sennūfer (Thebes West, N° 96). (PM, I,₁ sec. ed., 202,/38/).
2. Scene of adoration as vignette of the "Book of the Dead". First scene on the papyrus of Kha^c, owner of Theban tomb N° 8. Temp. Amenophis II-Amenophis III. Museo Egizio di Torino, N° Suppl. 8438. (E. Scamuzzi, L'art égyptien au Musée de Turin, Turin, 1966, pl. XLIX).

Plate XXXII

Goddess Ḥatḥor represented as cow. Deir el-Bahari, temple of Hatshepsut, shrine of Ḥatḥor. Reliefs with polychrome paintings. Limestone.
1. Ḥatḥor-cow licking hand of Queen Hatshepsut (cartouches changed to Tuthmosis II). (PM, II, 351,/33/, 2).
2. Cow-goddess suckling Queen Hatshepsut, with Amūn in front. (PM, II, 353/52/).

Plate XXXIII

Ḥatḥor shown as anthropomorphic deity. Tuthmosis III striking the ball before the goddess, with two priests holding balls. Deir el-Bahari, temple of Hatshepsut, shrine of Ḥatḥor. Relief with polychrome painting. (PM, II, 351,/38/).

Plate XXXIV

Goddess Wert-ḥekau in ritual scenes.
1. Wert-ḥekau showing her collar to Amūn. Deir el-Bahari, temple of Hatshepsut, shrine of Ḥatḥor. Relief with polychrome painting. (PM, II, 351,/37/).
2. The goddess crowning King Tuthmosis IV followed by Thoth. One of two analogous panels from sides of throne found in the tomb of Tuthmosis IV (Valley of the Kings, N° 43). Relief in wood. Metropolitan Museum of Art, New York, 30.8.45. (PM, I,₂, sec. ed., 561, finds).

Plate XXXV

Rites performed before goddesses. Reliefs in the tomb of Khaᶜemḥēt (Thebes West, N°
57). Temp. Amenophis III. Limestone.
1. Offering foreleg to Western goddess. (PM, I,₁, sec. ed., 117,/18/, I).
2. Offering on braziers to serpent-headed Termuthis, goddess of fertility, suckling King as
child. (Id. Ib., 114,/8/, II).

Plate XXXVI

The ritual of "opening the mouth". Reliefs in Theban tombs, temp. Amenophis III.
Limestone.
1. Statue of deceased purified and acclaimed by priests. Tomb of Raᶜmosi (Thebes West,
N° 55). (PM, I,₁, sec. ed., 109,/9/, II).
2. List of ritual instruments and jars used during ceremonies of "opening the mouth".
Lower part of stela in the court of the tomb of Khaᶜemḥēt (Thebes West, N° 57). (Id. Ib.,
114,/4/).

Plate XXXVII

Funeral rites. Polychrome paintings on a pillar in the tomb of Sennūfer (Thebes West, N°
96).
1. Purification of the deceased standing in an alabaster vessel. (PM, I,₁, sec. ed., 203,
pillar H/d/).
2. Deceased receiving pectorals from his wife. (Id. Ib., 203, pillar H/c/).

Plate XXXVIII

Burnt offerings. Reliefs in Theban tombs. Temp. Amenophis III. Limestone.
1. In the tomb of Khaᶜemḥēt (Thebes West, N° 57). (PM, I,₁, sec. ed., 116,/12/).
2. In the tomb of Raᶜmosi (Thebes West, N° 55). (Id. Ib., 107,/3/).

Plate XXXIX

Offering-rites in tombs of the nobles. Scenes on walls of Theban tombs.
1. Offering-table in front of the deceased. Polychrome painting in the tomb of Sennūfer
(Thebes West, N° 96). (PM, I,₁, sec. ed., 202,/39/).
2. Deceased offering on braziers and pouring myrrh upon offerings. Relief in the tomb of
Khaᶜemḥēt (Thebes West, N° 57). Limestone. (Id. Ib., 116,/12/).

Plate XL

"Sem"-priest performing funeral rites. Polychrome paintings on walls in the tomb of
Sennūfer (Thebes West, N° 96).
1. Purifying deceased and his wife. (PM, I,₁, sec. ed., 201,/36/).
2. Censing and libating at an offering-table before the deceased and his wife. (Id. Ib.,
201,/35/).

Plate XLI

Festival ceremonies attended by a Theban noble. Reliefs decorating walls in the tomb of
Khaᶜemḥēt (Thebes West, N° 57). Temp. Amenophis III. Limestone.

1. Tomb-owner decorated with cone of myrrh and with collar. (PM, I,₁, 116,/15/).
2. Tomb-owner and officials acclaiming King Amenophis III (fragment of scene). (Id. Ib., 116,/15/).

Plate XLII

"Pilgrimage to Abydos" as part of funeral ceremonies. Polychrome painting in the tomb of Sennūfer (Thebes West, N° 96). (PM, I,₁, sec. ed., 202,/40/, I-II).

Plate XLIII

Funeral rites. Reliefs on walls in the tomb of Khaᶜemḥēt (Thebes West, N° 57). Limestone.
1. Bark with statues of deceased and his wife—a scene of the "Abydos pilgrimage" to the tomb. (PM, I,₁, sec. ed., 118,/21/-/22 /).
2. Female mourners and a priest censing and libating in front of kiosk containing a bouquet—an allegory of death. (Id. Ib., 118,/21/-/22/, comp. E. Brovarski in JEA, 63, 1977, 178).

Plate XLIV

Ritual dances and games at royal festivities. Reliefs in the tomb of Kheruef (Thebes West, N° 192). Temp. Amenophis III to Amenophis IV. Limestone.
1. Male and female dancers. (PM, I,₁, sec. ed., 299/7/,II; The Epigraphic Survey, Chicago, pl. 59-63, text p. 62-3).
2. Men jousting with papyrus-stalks. (Id. Ib.).

Plate XLV

Personification of the Nile. Reliefs from Theban temples. Temp. Amenophis III. Limestone.
1. Nile-god standing on the "gold"-basket. Decoration of a column from the upper terrace in the temple of Hatshepsut at Deir al-Bahari. Block Nr. 366. (Z. Wysocki in JEA, 66, 1980, 58, fig. 2/N° 4/).
2. Nile-gods binding "sma"-symbols of Lower and Upper Egypt. Scene on side of throne. South "colossus of Memnon", north side. (PM, II, 450).
3. Part of a "geographical procession". Three nome-gods bearing offerings. Fragment of a polychrome relief, probably from a Theban temple. Dimensions: l.-77,2 cm; h.-42,3 cm. The Cleveland Museum of Art, N° 61.205. (J. D. Cooney in "The Bulletin of the Cleveland Museum of Art", November 1967, 280-1 and 1979, 338-341).

Plate XLVI

Cult of animal-gods. Votive stelae.
1. Adoration of the Heliopolitan bull Mnevis. Stela from Heliopolis. Probably temp. Amenophis III. Dimensions: h.- 45 cm; w.-30,8 cm. Egyptian Museum, Cairo, JE 65831. (Hildesheimer Ägyptologische Beiträge, V, 1978, 178-9, N° 6, pl. IX).
2. Bringing offerings to the crocodile-god Sobk. Stela from Dahamsha (ancient Sumenu), Upper Egypt. Probably temp. Amenophis III. Limestone. Dimensions: h.-110,5 cm;

w.-74,5 cm. Luxor Museum, J. 149. (Das Museum für Altägyptische Kunst in Luxor. Katalog, Mainz, 1981, 62, Nr. 79).

Plate XLVII

Monuments dedicated to the crocodile-god Sobk. From a temple of Sobk in Dahamsha (ancient Sumenu), Upper Egypt. Temp. Amenophis III.

1. Statue of two crocodiles on a socle decorated with reliefs. Black granit. Dimensions: h.-55,5 cm; w.-30 cm; d.-30,5 cm. Luxor Museum, J. 136. (Das Museum für Altägyptische Kunst in Luxor, Katalog, Mainz, 1981, 94-5, N° 123).

a) Nebnefer, a high official, adoring the name of Amenophis III beloved of Sobk.

b) Sistrum-emblem of goddess Hathor connected with the King's name—an example of decorative cryptography.

2. Statue of Sobk giving the symbol of life to the King. Calcite. Dimensions: h.-256,5 cm; w.-100 cm; d.-116 cm. Luxor Museum, J. 155. (Id. Ib., 82-4, N° 107).

Plate XLVIII

Religious items as hieroglyphic signs and as decorative elements. Details of reliefs in the tomb of Kheruef (Thebes West, N° 192). Limestone. Temp. Amenophis III.

1. Vase, collar and pectoral decorated with symbols of Lower and Upper Egypt, combined with a figure of the King and his names. (PM, $I_{,1}$, sec. ed., 299/8/; The Epigraphic Survey, Chicago, pl. 47-52 B).

2.-3. Hieroglyphic signs in a hymn to Rē͑: 2) goddess Ma͑et. 3) snake stuck with knives (PM, $I_{,1}$, sec. ed. 299/9/; The Epigraphic Survey, Chigago, pl. 73, 75-77 A, text p. 70-72).

1. Amosis. Limestone stela found in Karnak.

2. Amenophis III. Sandstone block from a Theban Temple.

Plate II   *The King as a heir of the falcon-god Horus*

2. Amenophis III protected by the falcon-god. Relief in the tomb of Kheruef

1. The falcon Behdety - a form of Horus. Relief of Amenophis I in Karnak

1. Nekhbet-bird as the crowning of a ritual scene. Relief in Karnak.

2. Queen Tetisheri wearing the vulture head-dress. Stela found in Abydos.

3. Queen Aḥmose. Relief in the temple of Hatshepsut.

Plate IV   *King Amenophis I offering to ityphallic Amūn-Rēᶜ*

1. Bread.

2. Scepter "sekhem".

3. Lettuce.

4. "Nu"-bowls.

1. Ḥeb-sed scene from a temple of Amenophis I in Karnak.

2. The coronation of Tuthmosis III. Relief on a pyramidion. Karnak.

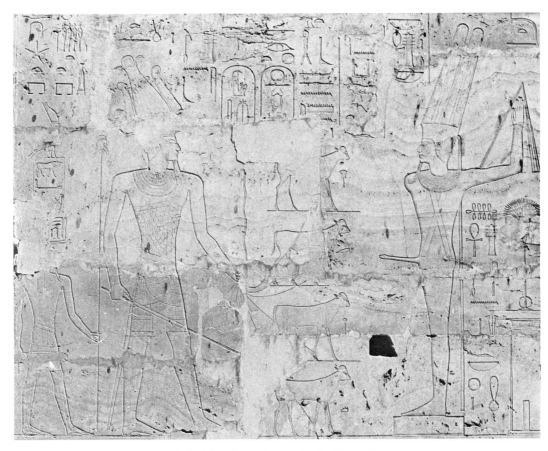

1. Driving four calves to Amūn-Kamutf.

2. Running with oar and ḥap-object.

3. Erecting the pole of a tent.

1. Hatshepsut. Karnak.

2. Tuthmosis III. Karnak.

Plate VIII   *Queen Hatshepsut with gods in ritual scenes. Karnak.*

1. Running with "ḥes"-vases to Amūn-Rēʿ.

2. With goddess Seshat in the rite of founding a temple.

1. Tuthmosis III rowing "Userhat" the river-bark of Amūn.

2. The portable bark-shrine leaving a bark-station.

3. Hatshepsut and Tuthmosis III **attending** a procession of the divine bark.

1. Hatshepsut offering two "nu"-jugs.

2. Hatshepsut running with the bull Apis to a bark-station.

3. Hatshepsut consecrating four "meret"-boxes.

1. Consecrating four "meret"-boxes.

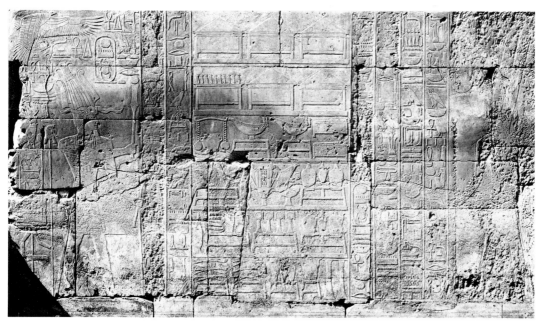

2. Dedicating treasure to Amūn.

Plate XII   *Scenes of daily ritual in the temple of Karnak.*

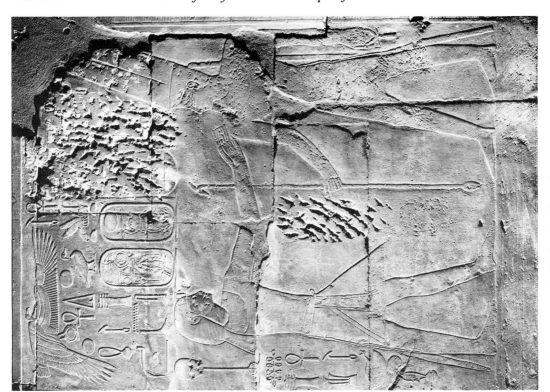

2. Tuthmosis II touching the god.

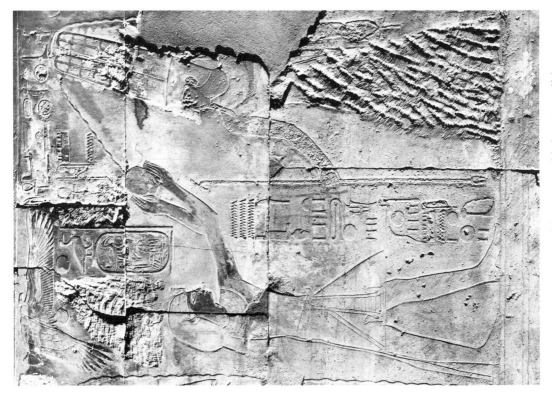

1. Tuthmosis II purifying Amūn with four "nmst"-jugs.

1. Purification with four "dšrt"-jugs.

2. Presenting incense to and pouring water on the statue.

Plate XIV   *Tuthmosis III censing. Karnak.*

1. Before the bark of Amūn standing in the fifth bark-station.

2. In front of god Ptah standing in his shrine.

2. The King embraced by the god.

1. Offering natron to the god.

2. Amenophis II embraced by the god.

1. Tuthmosis III led by god Monthu to Amūn giving life.

1. Block with names of Tuthmosis I, from above a door.

2. Religious motifs on the base of a royal shrine.

1. Tuthmosis III. VIIth pylon.

2. Amenophis II. VIIIth pylon.

Plate XX *The Egyptian King and his foreign enemies.*

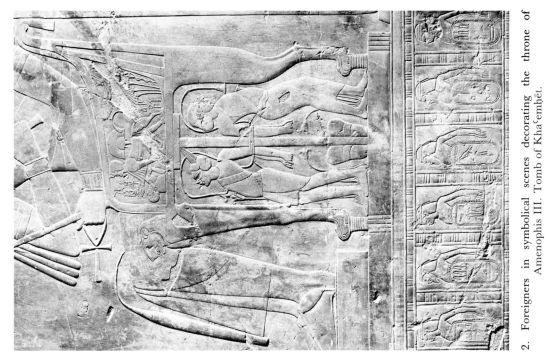

2. Foreigners in symbolical scenes decorating the throne of Amenophis III. Tomb of Khaᶜemḥēt.

1. Tuthmosis IV slaying captives. Relief decorating the chariot found in the King's tomb.

1. Tuthmosis IV represented as sphinx, trampling foes. Relief on the King's chariot.

2. Asiatic, Libyan and Nubian people with their ring-names. Tomb of Kheruef.

1. Royal family approaching the tree-goddess. Tomb of Tuthmosis III.

2. Statues of the royal family including Tuthmosis III and his wife. Karnak.

2. Deified Tuthmosis II receiving offerings.

1. Sesostris I and Tuthmosis III represented as parallel gods.

Plate XXIV　　　　　　*Processions of offering-bringers.*

1. Singers and priests with ritual objects in the Karnak temple.

2. Procession of men bringing funeral equipment. Tomb of Sennūfer.

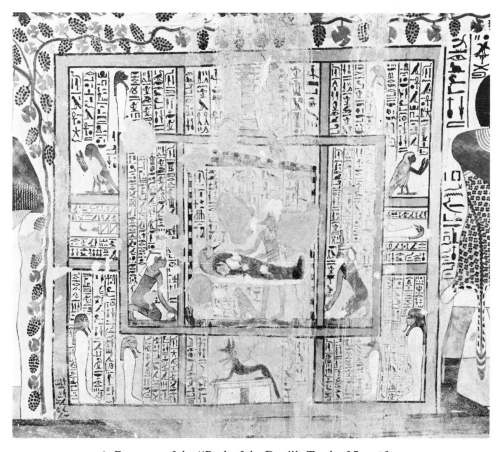

1. Fragment of the ''Book of the Dead''. Tomb of Sennūfer.

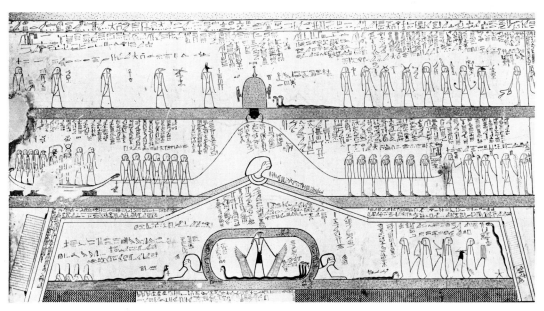

2. Fragment of the ''Amduat''. Tomb of Tuthmosis III.

Plate XXVI   *Divinities of the "Amduat". Tomb of Tuthmosis III.*

1. Flesh of Osiris.

2. Flesh of Atum.

3. Thoth.

4. God of many faces.

1.

2.

3.

4.

Plate XXVIII   *The world of the "Amduat". Tomb of Tuthmosis III.*

1. Dwellers of the other world in different attitudes.

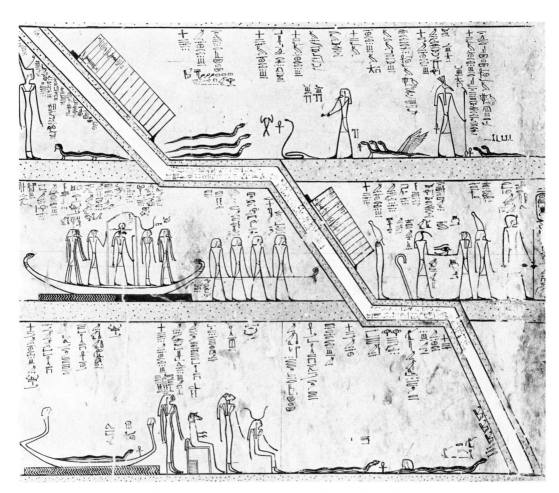

2. Sand-ways and water-basins in the fourth division.

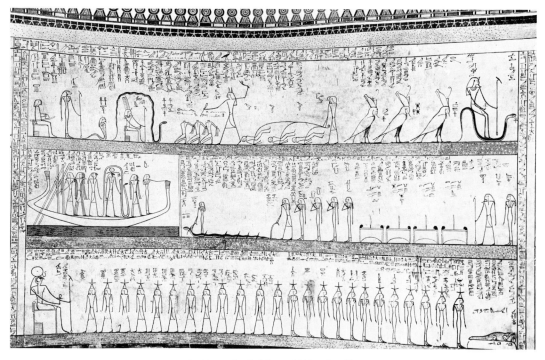

1. Seventh division of "Amduat".

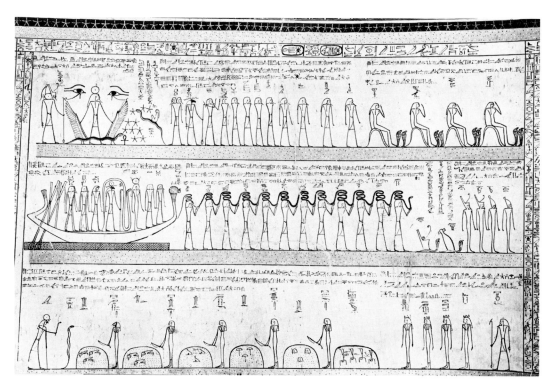

2. Eleventh division of "Amduat".

Plate XXX *Solar god and Osiris — two aspects of the other world.*

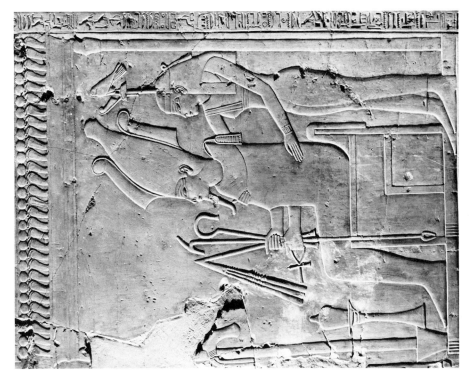

2. Osiris and the Western goddess. Tomb of the Khaʿemḥēt.

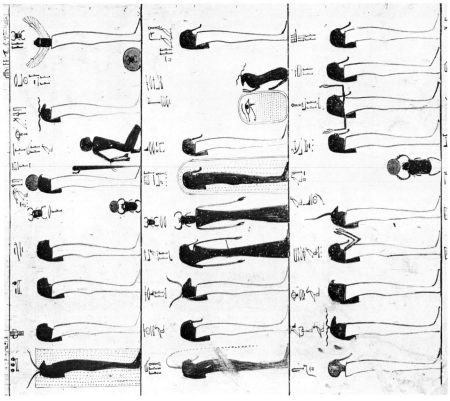

1. Forms of the solar deity. Tomb of Tuthmosis III.

1. Osiris and Anubis adored by tomb owner and his wife. Tomb of Sennūfer.

2. Scene of adoration as vignette of the "Book of the Dead". Papyrus of Khaᶜ.

1. Ḥathor-cow licking hand of Queen Hatshepsut.

2. Cow-goddess suckling Queen Hatshepsut.

Tuthmosis III striking the ball.

Plate XXXIV   *Goddess Wert-ḥekau in ritual scenes.*

2. The goddess crowning King Tuthmosis IV. Throne of Tuthmosis IV.

1. Wert-ḥekau showing her collar to Amūn. Deir el-Bahari.

1. Offering foreleg to Western goddess.

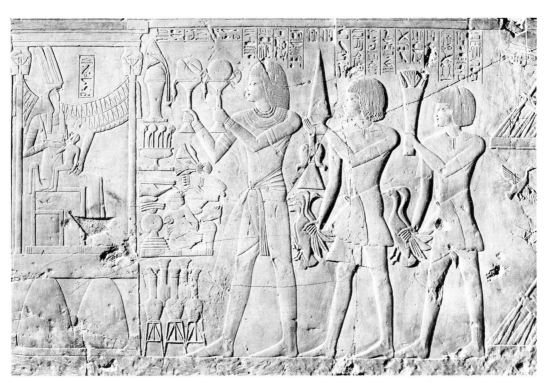

2. Offering on braziers to serpent-headed Termuthis.

1. Statue of deceased purified by priests. Tomb of Raʿmosi.

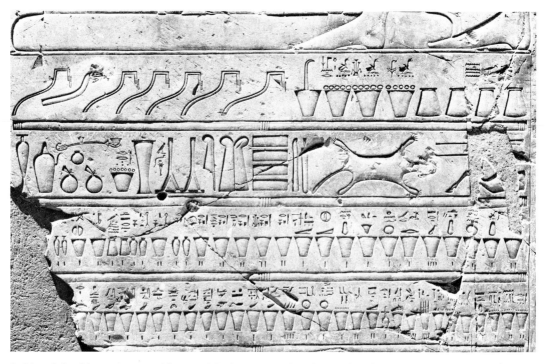

2. List of ritual instruments and jars used during ceremonies of "opening the mouth". Tomb of Khaʿemḥēt.

2. Deceased receiving pectorals.

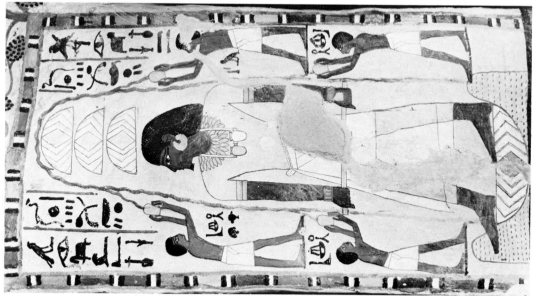

1. Purification of the deceased.

Plate XXXVIII   *Burnt offerings. Reliefs in Theban tombs.*

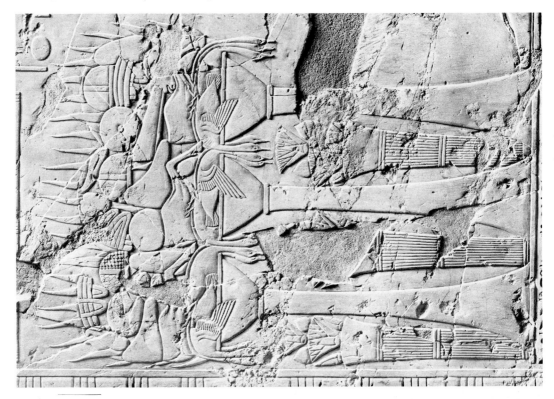

2. In the tomb of Raʿmosi.

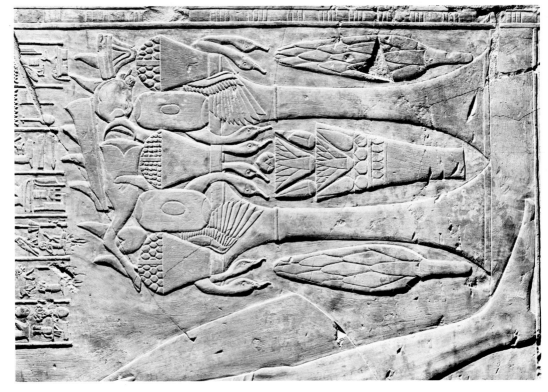

1. In the tomb of Khaʿemhēt.

1. Offering-table. Tomb of Sennūfer.

2. Deceased offering on braziers and pouring myrrh upon offerings. Tomb of Khaʿemḥēt.

2. Censing and libating at an offering-table.

1. Purifying deceased and his wife.

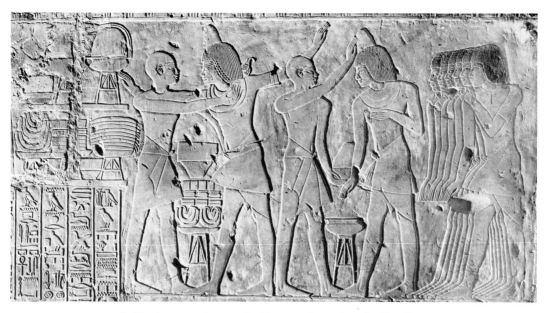

1. Tomb-owner decorated with cone of myrrh and with collar.

2. Tomb-owner and officials acclaiming King Amenophis III.

Plate XLII   *"Pilgrimage to Abydos"*

Painting in the tomb of Sennūfer.

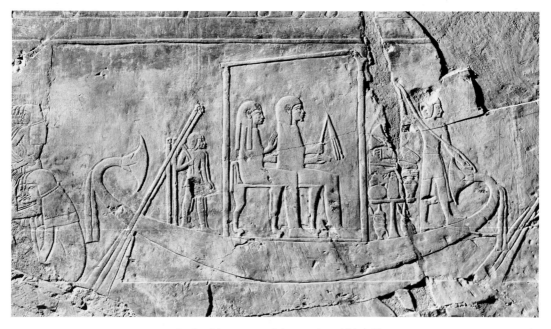

1. Bark with statues of deceased and his wife.

2. Female mourners and a priest censing and libating.

1. Male and female dancers.

2. Men jousting with papyrus-stalks.

1. Standing on the
   "gold"-basket.

2. Nile-gods binding "sma"-symbols.

3. Part of a "geographical procession". Three nome-gods.

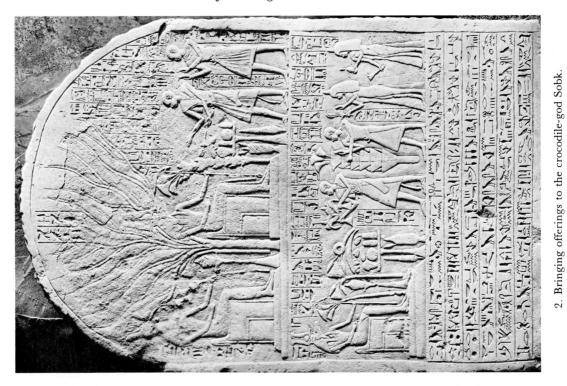

2. Bringing offerings to the crocodile-god Sobk.

1. Adoration of the Heliopolitan bull Mnevis.

a)

b)

1. Statue of two crocodiles.

a)

b)

2. Statue of Sobk giving the symbol of life to the King.

Plate XLVIII   *Religious items as hieroglyphic signs and as decorative elements.*

1. Vase, collar and pectoral decorated with symbols of Lower and Upper Egypt.

2. Goddess Maᶜet (hieroglyphic sign).

3. Snake stuck with knives (hieroglyphic sign).